Photography and the Law

Photography and the Law

A Practical Guide

Robert H. Ratcliffe

UNIVERSITY OF TORONTO PRESS
Toronto Buffalo London

Irwin Law
An imprint of University of Toronto Press
Toronto Buffalo London
utppublishing.com
Printed in Canada

ISBN 978-1-4875-6492-6 (paper)
ISBN 978-1-4875-6496-4 (EPUB)
ISBN 978-1-4875-6493-3 (PDF)

Library and Archives Canada Cataloguing in Publication

Title: Photography and the law : a practical guide / Robert H. Ratcliffe.
Names: Ratcliffe, Robert H., author.
Description: Includes bibliographical references and index.
Identifiers: Canadiana (print) 20250250446 | Canadiana (ebook) 20250250497 | ISBN 9781487564926 (paper) | ISBN 9781487564964 (EPUB) | ISBN 9781487564933 (PDF)
Subjects: LCSH: Photography – Law and legislation – Canada. | LCSH: Copyright – Photographs – Canada.
Classification: LCC KE2868.R38 2025 kfmod | LCC KF3050 .R38 2025 | DDC 343.7107/877 – dc23

Cover design: Em Dash Design
Cover images: BCFC/Shutterstock.com; Triff/Shutterstock.com; trevor-hayes/Unsplash

We wish to acknowledge the land on which the University of Toronto Press operates. This land is the traditional territory of the Wendat, the Anishnaabeg, the Haudenosaunee, the Métis, and the Mississaugas of the Credit First Nation.

University of Toronto Press acknowledges the financial support of the Government of Canada, the Canada Council for the Arts, and the Ontario Arts Council, an agency of the Government of Ontario, for its publishing activities.

FSC
www.fsc.org
MIX
Paper | Supporting responsible forestry
FSC® C013916

To Lisa, whose unwavering belief in me has been the foundation of my every success

Summary Table of Contents

Detailed Table of Contents

1

Introduction

Freezing Time

From the humble beginnings of the camera in the 1800s, to the ever-present smartphones equipped with high-resolution cameras today, the act of capturing moments in time has become an intrinsic part of our daily lives.

The dawn of photography brought a revolution in human expression offering a means to immortalize fleeting moments and preserve them for future generations. From the earliest images recorded on metal plates and glass, to the digital images of today, photography has evolved into a powerful tool for communication, artistry, and memory.

Digital technology has democratized the act of photography, empowering individuals worldwide to capture and share their experiences with ease. With the tap of a screen, we can record historic moments, tell stories, and convey emotions in ways that words often cannot. Photography invites us to explore the world around us and preserve those fleeting moments that will never happen again.

Legal Issues in Photography

Underneath the art of photography lies a set of legal principles that shape how we document our world. This book looks at the key legal considerations and covers the best practices you should follow to ensure your work complies with the law.

We will guide you through the rules that apply to various places you take photographs. Knowing the differences between public spaces, publicly accessible private property, and strictly private property is important. For example, in public places, you have wide discretion to take photographs, but some restrictions may apply. In locations like shopping malls or sports stadiums, which are privately owned but open to the public, rules may require that you get permission. On private property, you will need the property owner's consent to take photographs. Appreciating these distinctions will help you steer clear of problems.

Understanding your rights under the *Copyright Act* is essential. This Act automatically gives photographers exclusive rights to reproduce, distribute, and display their work, protecting it from unauthorized use. For instance, if someone wants to use your photograph, they need your permission because you hold the exclusive rights over how that image can be used.

Photographers' rights often intersect with others' rights. For example, if your photograph includes copyrighted material, you need to consider the original creator's rights. Similarly, when photographing identifiable people, you must balance their privacy rights with your freedom of expression rights. Property owners' rights also come into play, and we will discuss how to navigate these overlapping rights.

Licensing and assigning your images are key concepts for managing and profiting from your intellectual property rights. Licensing allows you to grant usage rights while maintaining ownership of the image. With an assignment you are transferring your ownership rights to someone else. We will explore how to negotiate and draft these agreements to protect your interests.

Despite their best efforts, photographers may fall victim to copyright infringement. Knowing the legal remedies available to protect your work, such as issuing cease and desist letters or pursuing legal action, helps protect your work. In addition, understanding how to avoid infringing on others' copyrights is equally important. This means being aware of fair use provisions and seeking permission when necessary. Familiarity with both protection and prevention will help you safeguard your rights and respect the work of others.

Different types of photography present unique legal challenges. For example, street photographers must navigate issues such as privacy in public, while wildlife photographers need to comply with conservation laws that protect habitats and species. Understanding the specific legal issues associated with different photography types will equip you with the knowledge you need to ensure your practices are both legal and ethical.

We will also discuss the types of legal actions photographers can face and how to avoid them. Taking photographs of someone in a private setting without permission, for example, or using copyrighted material without authorization can result in litigation. Understanding the legal basis for these actions and taking steps to avoid them will reduce your risk of landing in a legal proceeding.

Proactive risk management is also essential if you want to minimize your legal risks. This includes acquiring appropriate insurance to protect against legal claims and financial losses. We will cover the different types of insurance that are beneficial, such as professional liability and equipment insurance, and how to incorporate risk management into your daily practice.

For a photographer, adopting an ethical approach to your craft means more than simply complying with legal requirements. It involves ensuring your work demonstrates respect for the people you photograph. For example, this includes obtaining their informed consent and being sensitive to cultural differences. By committing to these ethical practices, you lay the groundwork for a distinguished career and produce work that resonates deeply with those who view it.

We will discuss all these issues in detail in this book.

Types of Photography

We take photographs for many reasons and will look at the three most common types of photography: personal, editorial, and commercial. Understanding the legal rights and rules for each type is crucial to ensure compliance with the law.

Personal use is the first category. Photography provides a wonderful outlet for self-expression, creativity, and personal enjoyment. Whether you are photographing family gatherings, travel adventures, or everyday moments, photography allow us to preserve special memories and reflect on our lives. Photographs for personal use are typically shared with family and friends and displayed in personal places like your home or office. Personal use does not involve commercial exploitation of the photograph, or any form of editorial sharing.

Editorial use[1] is the next category. This type of photography plays an important role in informing and educating society. Photographs used in newspapers, magazines, online news platforms, blogs, and social media, serve as a visual storytelling tool that complements the written record. By capturing current events, social issues, cultural trends, and human experiences, editorial photographs help shape our understanding of the world around us.

Commercial photography is the third category and serves a different purpose. It is a powerful tool for businesses and organizations to showcase their products, services, and brands. The aim is to create appealing visual images that attract the public, boost sales, and build brand loyalty. Commercial photographs are used in various contexts, such as

---

1 "Editorial" is the term that will be used throughout where the photograph is shared publicly in news articles, magazines, blogs, or other media outlets to inform, educate, or comment on a newsworthy event, topic, or issue, and on social media sites such as Facebook, Instagram, or X (formerly known as Twitter).

e-commerce websites, print advertisements, billboards, company websites, social media profiles, product packaging, and catalogues.

This book is intended as a guide to help you understand the array of legal issues photographers face today. Laws change, and it is important to stay up to date on new rules and industry practices. This book does not constitute legal advice, and if you are uncertain about your legal rights or obligations, you should consult with your own lawyer or legal expert. A professional well-versed in intellectual property law, property law, privacy law, and relevant legislation will be able to provide the assistance you need. Staying informed will ensure you can navigate the legal landscape of photography confidently.

2

Shooting Locations

Overview

We will start by exploring the various locations where you may take photographs and the specific rules and considerations that apply to each. Understanding these distinctions is crucial for staying within legal boundaries and avoiding potential problems. Different locations, whether public spaces, private properties, or special venues, each have their own set of expectations and rules.

Public Places

Generally, there are no limitations on taking photographs in public locations. Public places include streets and sidewalks, parks, town squares, and government buildings that are open to the public. However, you may encounter certain sites where there is an express prohibition such as a sign that says no photography allowed in a particular area. You must follow this direction.

Photographing people in public places is generally permitted without the need for consent, because individuals in public spaces typically have a lower expectation of privacy. However, photographers should still be mindful of privacy concerns, especially when capturing images of individuals in situations where there might be a reasonable expectation of privacy.[1]

There are other exceptions where privacy considerations come into play. For instance, capturing images from a public space through a window into someone's home or into their backyard, violates their privacy rights. This rule also applies to locations like public restrooms, where taking photographs would violate someone's privacy. These examples emphasize the need to honour privacy rights, even in public places.

You are allowed to take pictures of fires, accidents, and law enforcement officers executing their duties from a public place. A police officer does not have legal authority to prevent you from photographing police activity. In *R v Zarafonitis*[2] an officer used excessive force arresting a photographer who was taking pictures of an altercation in a bar. The court found that unless the photographer's "presence or actions were creating a danger to him or others, ordering him to stop photographing was not a lawful command."[3]

---

1 See *Aubry v Éditions Vice-Versa Inc* [1998] 1 SCR 591.
2 2013 ONCJ 570.
3 *Ibid* at para 24.

However, a police officer is permitted to respond to any overarching safety concerns and can order you to back away if there is danger in being too close, or you are impeding emergency personnel from doing their jobs. Always be thoughtful as you go about taking your photographs. You do not want to risk an injury to yourself or cause harm to someone else.

Some cities and municipalities require a permit and charge a fee if you are doing certain types of photography in public places such as parks. For example, in Toronto parks, a permit is required for commercial photography of any kind. This includes photo shoots like wedding or graduation ceremonies.[4]

When shooting in a public place, it is wise to check for any laws that are specific to photography in that location. Laws will vary from city to city, and province to province. If you're unsure, it is sensible and courteous to ask whether taking photographs is allowed in that public area.

Public Places – Private Property

You are generally allowed to take pictures on private property that is open to the public. This includes places like shopping malls, stores, amusement parks, restaurants, sports venues, and hotels. However, property owners have the right to establish the rules for taking photographs on

---

4 Toronto Municipal Code, c 608, Parks: "§ 608-47. Filming and videotaping. While in a park, no person shall take or permit to be taken for remuneration any film, photograph, videotape, or television broadcast unless permitted under the City's film by-law 56 and authorized by permit from the Toronto Film and Television Office."

their premises. For example, in the public areas of downtown Toronto office buildings, it is not uncommon for security personnel, if they see you with a camera, to approach and inform you that taking photographs is not allowed. Pay attention to any signs or posted policies regarding photography. If there are no signs that limit the taking of photographs, you are free to take pictures until you are instructed to stop by the owner or security personnel. If asked to stop or leave, do so courteously and promptly to avoid any further issues.

Many sports stadiums in Canada, such as Scotiabank Arena and Rogers Centre, have specific restrictions on photography to ensure the safety and enjoyment of all attendees. For instance, non-flash still photography is generally permitted, but the use of professional-grade equipment with lenses longer than 75mm is prohibited.[5] There are different reasons for these rules. By limiting the use of large, obtrusive equipment, venues can ensure that all spectators have an unobstructed view and can fully enjoy the event without distractions. In addition, sports venues often have exclusive contracts with professional photographers and broadcasters. Allowing professional-grade equipment into the venue could encroach on these agreements and lead to unauthorized commercial use of images.

To avoid any problems, it is a good idea to ask about the photography rules as soon as you arrive. Asking security staff for clarification can help you avoid misunderstandings,

5 *Rogers Centre Information Guide 2024.*

and ensure you are following the property owner's guidelines. Even if you are in a public area, the property owner has the right to set and enforce their own rules. By following their rules, you can take photographs and maintain a good relationship with those in charge of the space.

Private Property

If you are planning on taking photographs on private property, you are subject to any restrictions the owner imposes. There can be serious consequences if you go onto private property without the owner's permission. For example, trespassing on private property is an offence under the *Trespass to Property Act* (*Trespass Act*) in Ontario.[6] Trespassing and failing to leave immediately upon request can result in your arrest and trespassing charges against you.[7] School Boards also have all the rights of a private property owner when access to a school property is involved.[8]

One ordinarily thinks of "private property" in conjunction with the word "land." However, in addition to land and buildings on land, Ontario's *Trespass Act* expands the definition of premises to include water, ships and vessels,

---

6 *Trespass to Property Act*, RSO 1990, c T.21, s 2(1); other provinces have similar legislation: *Trespass Act*, RSBC 2018, c 3; *Petty Trespass Act*, RSA 2000, c P-11; and *Protection of Property Act*, RSNS 1989, c 363.

7 Section 9(1) "A police officer, or the occupier of premises, or a person authorized by the occupier may arrest without warrant any person he or she believes on reasonable and probable grounds to be on the premises in contravention of section 2."

8 Section 1(2).

trailers and portable structures used for a residence, business or shelter, trains, railway cars, and vehicles and aircraft, except while in operation.[9]

There are different ways the owner can notify you of trespass. They can give you notice of their position orally, in writing, or by way of signs. If the owner posts a "No Trespassing" sign at the edge of the property, you should not enter the property. Under the Ontario *Trespass Act* entry is prohibited even without "notice" if the premises is a garden, field, or other land under cultivation. This includes a lawn, orchard, vineyard, woodlots on land used primarily for agricultural purposes, and fenced in areas.[10] If the owner permits you to enter onto the property, they are free to restrict where you can go and what you do there. For example, the owner may authorize hiking through a vineyard, provided you stay on a particular trail when you are taking photographs.

Under the *Trespass Act* a conviction can result in a fine of up to $10,000.[11] If you cause any damage to the property, the owner may also bring a civil action in court to recover money for the damage you have caused.[12]

To avoid any problems, the first and best approach is to contact the owner and ask for permission to enter their premises. If the owner does not impose any restrictions on where you can go or what you can photograph, you are free

9 Section 1(1).
10 Section 3(1).
11 Section 2(1).
12 Section 12(1).

of any worries. For example, if you are a photographer who likes to capture stars in the night-time sky, it may be necessary to take your late-night shots from the middle of a farmer's field. Do not be afraid to meet with the farmer and explain what you want to do. Offering to provide the property owner with a copy of some your photographs can often help smooth the way.

Special Locations

In Canada there are several places where individuals have a reasonable expectation of privacy. Photographers must be vigilant about obtaining express consent if you want to take photographs in these locations.

Religious Institutions

The beauty of the architecture in some of the world's oldest places of worship is stunning. As a photographer, respecting privacy in places of worship is crucial because these places are not just buildings, they are sacred spaces where people worship and connect with their faith. Whether you are photographing temples, churches, mosques, or synagogues, you should ask for permission before you take any photographs. Sensitivity is key. If a religious service or prayer is in progress, be quiet and do not take photographs unless this is allowed. Ensure you set your camera to silent mode. Many places of worship have specific guidelines about when and where photography is allowed, especially during religious ceremonies.[13] Always respect these guidelines. Taking photographs outside the building should not present a problem but keep in mind the sanctity of your surroundings.

Hospitals

Many hospitals have policies to protect the privacy and confidentiality of patients, staff, and visitors.[14] These policies may restrict or prohibit photography on hospital premises, especially in sensitive areas such as patients' rooms, operating rooms, and emergency departments. Sometimes hospitals have rules regarding the use of photography for commercial or promotional purposes within their facilities. Before you take any pictures at a hospital you should find out what guidelines and restrictions are in place.

Schools

Schools usually have policies governing photography on school property to protect the privacy and safety of students and staff.[15] These policies can regulate who may take photographs, for what purpose, and where within the school facilities the photographs can be taken.[16] You should check

---

13 For example, the Basilica of Our Lady Immaculate in Guelph, Ontario.

14 Toronto General Hospital has policies prohibiting photography and recording without prior authorization, except for authorized personnel conducting hospital business.

15 A school board also has the rights of an occupier in respect of its school sites under the *Trespass to Property Act*, RSO 1990, c T.21, s 1(2).

16 The Toronto District School Board has guidelines regarding photography and video recording on school property which requires individuals to obtain

with the school board to see what policies exist before taking any photographs on school property or in a school. For example, the Toronto District School Board (TDSB) requires consent forms to be signed by parents or guardians before students can be photographed or recorded. Always be respectful of privacy and safety concerns and comply with any requests to stop taking photographs and delete your images if asked to do so.

Courtrooms

The rules for photography in courtrooms vary across Canada. In Ontario members of the public are not allowed to use a camera in a courtroom unless the judge makes an order allowing that. British Columbia has an additional requirement before a camera can be used. You cannot take a photograph during a court proceeding unless the judge authorizes you, and the parties to the legal proceeding, consent.[17] In Alberta a member of the public is not permitted to use a camera in the courtroom at all. Different rules apply to lawyers and the media in most cases.

The Supreme Court of Canada in Ottawa allows you to take pictures in the public areas of the Supreme Court building, including the main lobby, and the courtroom when the Court is not sitting. These photographs can only be taken

---

permission from school administrators before taking photographs or recording video during school events or activities.

17 In British Columbia, the "Policy on Use of Electronic Devices in Courtrooms," effective since 17 September 2012, governs the use of cameras and other electronic devices in courtrooms.

for personal use or educational purposes unless the deputy registrar gives you permission to use them for commercial or promotional purposes.

It is important to identify what rules apply in your Province or Territory and carefully follow those rules if you want to avoid the possibility of trouble with the court.

Summary

The rules that apply when you are taking photographs depend on your location. When you are on public property, you generally have the freedom to photograph whatever you want, although there are some restrictions involving privacy rights about which you need to be aware. For private property with public access, you must follow the property owner's rules in the public areas. On private property, you need permission from the owner to take photographs on the property, and you must also comply with any additional rules the owner imposes. There are also several places where individuals have a reasonable expectation of privacy, and special rules apply. Understanding these distinctions is essential if you want to ensure you are complying with the law.

3
Copyright Law

Overview

Understanding copyright law is crucial for anyone working in the creative fields. Knowing the basics will help you protect your work and ensure that you are not violating the rights of others.

Copyright law came into existence in England in 1709. In Canada copyright law falls within the federal jurisdiction and the Parliament of Canada passed the first *Copyright Act* in 1924. "Copyright" essentially means "the right to copy." If you hold the copyright, you have the sole right to produce or reproduce a work or a substantial part of it.

The *Copyright Act*[1] is federal legislation that applies across Canada in all the provinces and territories. Copyright law

1 RSC 1985, c C-42.

is designed to foster and encourage creativity by rewarding creators of original works. Under the Act, copyright exists in every original literary, dramatic, musical, and artistic work. In 2012, photographs were added to the term "artistic work" and photographs are protected in the same way as other artistic works. Because copyright is created under a statute, the *Copyright Act* addresses all the legal aspects of copyright, subject to the court's interpretation of the Act's provisions. In other words, the rights and remedies set out in the statute are exhaustive.[2]

Copyright protects how an idea is expressed artistically, not the idea itself. For example, consider the Golden Gate Bridge in San Francisco that millions of people have photographed. To be protected by copyright, the photograph must be "original." Originality requires the photographer to use some level of "skill and judgment" in creating the photograph, which involves more than just copying another photograph. While each photographer might capture the same "bridge," their unique way of framing, lighting, and interpreting the scene is what is protected. At the same time, the photograph does not need to be "novel or unique" to qualify as original.[3]

Copyright Ownership

With certain limited exceptions, the person who takes the photograph becomes the copyright owner the instant the picture is taken. This includes those situations where

---

2 *CCH Canadian Ltd v Law Society of Upper Canada* 2004 SCC 13 at para 22.
3 *Ibid* at para 16.

the photographer is commissioned to take the pictures at a wedding, for example, or for some other special occasion.

One exception arises where the photographer is an employee or apprentice and makes the photograph in the course of their employment. In that situation, the employer is the first owner of the copyright, subject to any agreement with the employee that may provide otherwise.[4] Another exception is where the photograph is created by or under the direction of the government of Canada or a provincial government, unless the parties agree otherwise.[5]

Copyright Term

If you are taking a photograph in Canada, Canadian law applies. Following a trade agreement Canada entered into with the United States and Mexico on 30 September 2018, copyright duration was extended from the life of the photographer plus fifty years, to life of the photographer plus seventy years. This change came into effect in Canada at the end of 2022.[6] For example, if a photograph was taken on 3 March 2018, and the photographer dies on 7 November 2035, the copyright protection would continue until the end of 2035, plus seventy additional years. After the copyright expires the image moves into what is called the public domain and

4 *Copyright Act*, s 13(3).

5 See s 12 of the *Copyright Act*. Also see *Keatley Surveying Ltd v Teranet Inc* 2017 ONCA 748.

6 The change to extend the copyright duration in Canada from fifty years to seventy years took effect on 30 December 2022.

may be freely copied and distributed without permission or payment of any royalties.

Rights Protected by Copyright

In *Théberge v Galerie d'Art du Petit Champlain inc*,[7] the Supreme Court of Canada established a key principle regarding the interpretation of the *Copyright Act*: the importance of balancing the rights of copyright owners with the public's interest in accessing and using creative works.

In this case, the issue was whether transferring an image from a paper poster to a canvas constituted "reproduction" of the copyrighted work. The Court found that it did not because there was no multiplication of the image. The original image was simply relocated. This interpretation limited the scope of copyright, supporting the view that copyright should protect only actual reproductions or copies, not every instance of image use, to avoid overly restricting public use and access.

The Court held that the *Copyright Act* is designed not only to protect the economic rights of creators by allowing them to control reproduction, but also to promote the broader public interest in the dissemination and enjoyment of artistic works. Therefore, copyright protection should not be interpreted in a way that unnecessarily limits public access or hinders the use of creative works.

---

7 [2002] 2 SCR 336.

This principle from *Théberge* has become a foundational guideline emphasizing that copyright should strike a balance between protecting creators and encouraging public engagement with creative content.

Economic Rights

Copyright protects two kinds of rights: (1) economic rights and (2) moral rights.

Economic rights allow the copyright owner to earn money if others use their image. The owner has the exclusive right to decide whether the work can be reproduced, and in what ways it may be used. The owner is also free to license or assign the copyrighted image. There are certain exceptions such as the fair dealing principle, which allows a person to use your copyrighted image without your permission.

Moral Rights

In addition to economic rights, the *Copyright Act* also grants the artist what are called "moral rights" in the work. Moral rights are distinct from the photographer's economic rights. Moral rights protect the personality or reputation of the artist by preventing another person from making changes to the photograph that would affect the "integrity of the work" in a negative way.

The definition of moral rights under the *Copyright Act* reflects the minimum requirements set by the Berne Convention for the Protection of Literary and Artist Works.[8] The Berne Convention of which Canada is a member provides that:

> A.1.1. (1) Independently of the author's economic rights, and even after the transfer of the said rights, the author shall have the right to claim authorship of the work and to object to any distortion, mutilation, or other modification of, or other derogatory action in relation to, the said work, which would be prejudicial to his honour or reputation.[9]

Moral rights provide limits on what a purchaser or assignee can do with the photograph. There are two distinct rights: the right of paternity and the right of integrity. The paternity right is the creator's right to be associated with the work by name, under a pseudonym, or even to remain anonymous.[10] The integrity right is infringed if the work is "distorted, mutilated or otherwise modified" or "used in association with a product, service, cause or institution" to the prejudice of the creator.[11]

In other words, the creator, even if no longer the owner of the work, can exercise control over how the work is presented. Moral rights are not assignable but in Canada you can waive these rights.[12] The duration of moral rights is the

8 In Canada, the Berne Convention's provisions are implemented through the *Copyright Act*, which aligns Canadian copyright law with the Convention's requirements.

9 Article 6bis(1).

10 *Copyright Act*, s 14.1(1).

11 *Folkes v Greensleeves Publishing Ltd* 1997 CanLII 12373 at para 10 (Ont SC).

12 Section 14.1(2) of the *Copyright Act* allows the waiver of moral rights in whole or in part, but the waiver must be in writing.

same as for copyright, the lifetime of the photographer plus seventy years.

Caselaw Illustrating Moral Rights

What do the words "distorted, mutilated or otherwise modified" mean? The court had to consider whether the plaintiff's moral rights were infringed by the defendants in *Snow v The Eaton Centre Ltd et al.*[13] In 1979 Michael Snow, a Canadian artist, was commissioned to create a sculpture for the Eaton Centre in Toronto. The sculpture hanging from the ceiling of the Eaton Centre consisted of sixty Canada geese in flight. In 1982 the marketing director at the Eaton Centre developed a plan that involved attaching red ribbons to the necks of the geese for the Christmas shopping season. Snow was never consulted and did not consent to this. Snow brought an action seeking to have the ribbons removed.

The court found that even though the Eaton Centre had commercial rights to the sculpture, Snow held moral rights to the artwork and the ribbons were prejudicial to his honour and reputation. In reaching this conclusion the court applied a two-part test with a subjective and an objective component. The subjective component addressed the creator's subjective perspective and the objective component considered whether that perspective was reasonably arrived at. In addition to Snow's evidence about his feelings of upset and frustration, other experts in the field addressed

13 (1982) 70 CPR (2d) 105.

the objective component and testified there was prejudice to Snow's honour and reputation by adding the ribbons.

Another case that addressed the scope of moral rights is *Richie v Sawmill Creek Golf & Country Club.*[14] In *Richie* the plaintiff alleged the defendants harmed him by making enlargements of his photographs that were so poor in quality they were "horrifying." The court found that the defendants had enlarged the plaintiff's photographs from prints rather than from negatives, and in doing so, had modified his original photographs. However, the court found that the plaintiff did not meet the test to establish that his work had been distorted, mutilated, or otherwise modified to the prejudice of his reputation.[15]

Exceptions to Copyright Infringement

Fair Dealing

In certain cases, a person can make copies of your copyrighted photographs and use them without obtaining permission or paying you.

Section 29 of the *Copyright Act* provides for a statutory exception called "fair dealing." The fair dealing exception allows a copyright protected works to be used without permission from, or payment to the copyright owner. The purpose of this exception is to balance the interests of the copyright owner with those of the public.

---

14 (2004) 189 OAC 282 (Div Ct).

15 There was no evidence to support the objective component.

To determine whether the use of the photograph falls under the fair dealing exception, courts apply a two-part test. First, the photograph must be used for research, private study, criticism, review, news reporting, education, satire, or parody. Second, the photograph must be used in a "fair" manner. A commercial purpose does not preclude the use of the fair dealing provisions. It is simply one element to be weighed in the overall fairness analysis.[16] The person relying upon the fair dealing exception has the onus of establishing that the test has been met.

In *CCH Canadian Ltd v Law Society of Upper Canada*,[17] the Supreme Court of Canada had to consider whether the Law Society of Upper Canada's photocopying service, which allowed lawyers and legal researchers to obtain copies of legal materials for research purposes, fell under the fair dealing exception. CCH Canadian Ltd, the publisher, argued that the Law Society's photocopying service infringed its copyright in various legal texts. The Supreme Court considered the application of section 29 and concluded the copying of the legal materials fell under the fair dealing exception because it was being used for research or private study. The Supreme Court set out six factors that need to be considered when deciding whether the use of a copyrighted work meets the test.[18] No single factor will determine the

16 See *CCH Canadian Ltd v Law Society of Upper Canada 2004* SCC 13 at para 54: "some dealings, even if for an allowable purpose, may be more or less fair than others; research done for commercial purposes may not be as fair as research done for charitable purposes."

17 [2004] 1 SCR 339.

18 *Ibid* at paras 54–60; for a case in which the Federal Court of Appeal found that the action taken did not constitute fair dealing, see York *University v Access Copyright* 2020 FAC 77.

question of fair dealing. In each case the answer depends on the facts and how the work is being used.

First, you look at the purpose for which the copyrighted work is being used.[19] Does it fall within one of the allowable purposes: research, private study, criticism, review, news reporting, education, satire, and parody?

Second, you consider the character of the dealing.[20] How is the copyrighted work being used? For example, if large numbers of copies of the work are being distributed, this may point to unfairness. In contrast, if a single copy or only a few copies of the work are used for a specific purpose, this would support the fair dealing argument.

Third, what amount of the copyrighted work is being used?[21] If the amount of the work taken is trivial, this does not support a case for infringement. However, in some cases there may be a legitimate reason for taking the whole of the work, as in the case of a photograph.

Fourth, you consider alternatives that are available instead of using the copyrighted work.[22] Were other alternatives available? Perhaps. Could a non-copyrighted equivalent have been used, or was it even necessary to use the original work?

Fifth, what is the nature of the work? The court considers whether there is a "public interest" in having the work widely disseminated. If the work serves a public benefit,

---

19 *Ibid* at para 54.
20 *Ibid* at para 55.
21 *Ibid* at para 56.
22 *Ibid* at para 57.

such as contributing to public knowledge or discourse, this could support a finding that the dealing is fair. If the work is confidential or private, this may weigh against a finding of fair dealing. For example, what if the work contains sensitive or proprietary information?[23]

Sixth, what is the effect on the original work?[24] Will the use compete with or adversely affect the original work in some way? If the reproduced work competes in the market with the original work, this may be unfair. Courts have said that the "fair dealing" exception to copyright infringement should not be interpreted restrictively.

In what kind of scenario might the fair dealing exception apply? Suppose a professional photographer specializing in wildlife photography has captured photographs of various wildlife species in their natural habitat. As the photographer, they hold the copyright in these photographs. A high school teacher preparing a lesson on ecology and biodiversity sees them online and decides to incorporate some of the pictures into the lesson to enrich the learning experience for the class. Can the teacher rely upon the fair dealing exception to use the photographs in the lessons without the photographer's consent?

The "purpose" of the dealing is educational in that the photographs are to be used in a biology class to facilitate learning. The use of the images is directly related to the educational objectives of the teacher's lesson. What is the "character of the dealing"? The number of the photographs

23 *Ibid* at para 58.
24 *Ibid* at para 59.

to be used is limited to a few select ones relevant to the lesson being taught. The teacher is not using all or even a substantial portion of the photographer's work. The creative and informative images will contribute to educational objectives of the lesson. Are there "alternatives" to using the photographer's images? Maybe. The teacher could explore the availability of other educational resources such as photographs in the public domain or consider licensed stock photographs. However, alternatives may not be readily available or may not meet the educational needs as well. The "effect" of using a few of the photographs for educational purposes is unlikely to have any significant impact on the market for the photographer's work. They are being used in a non-commercial educational context that does not complete with the photographer's primary market.

Given the facts in this case, a court would likely find that the teacher's use of the photographs qualifies under the fair dealing provision in the *Copyright Act*. The educational purpose for using the photographs, the limited nature of the usage, and the minimal impact on the market for the photographer's work support the application of the fair dealing provisions. It is essential to remember that the fair dealing exemption is fact based, and each case must be determined on its own merits.

Private Purposes

Section 29.22(1) of the *Copyright Act* also provides an exception from copyright infringement. Under section 29.22(1) an individual can reproduce a copyrighted work without it being considered copyright infringement provided that the copy of the work being used to make the reproduction must not be an infringing copy. In other words, it is a legitimate, legally obtained copy. Second, you must have legally obtained the original copy of the work,[25] and you must own or be authorized to use the device or medium on which you reproduce the work. Third, you must not have bypassed any digital locks or technological protection measures that protect the work, as defined in section 41 of the Act. Fourth, you cannot give away the reproduction to others. It must remain with you. Finally, the reproduction must be used only for your private purposes. This means it must not be shared publicly or used for a commercial purpose.

What kind of fact situation would section 29.22(1) apply to? Suppose a photographer who enjoys creating digital art legally purchases a high-resolution digital image of a classic painting from an authorized online art store. The photographer wants to use this image as part of a new digital art project they are working on, and plan to combine the painting with the original photographs to create a new piece for their personal portfolio.

Does this comply with the wording of section 29.22(1)? The digital image of the classic painting the photographer purchased is a legitimate, non-infringing copy. They obtained it from an authorized online art store that sells licensed digital images of classic paintings and downloaded it to their computer. They own the computer and use it for

25 It was not borrowed or rented.

creating and storing their digital art projects. There was no need to bypass any digital locks or technological protection measures to download and use the image. The file was provided in an accessible format by the online store. They keep the final digital art project on their personal computer and do not sell prints of the artwork or use it for any commercial purpose. Finally, the digital art project is used solely for the photographer's private purposes.

In summary, the photographer's actions comply with section 29.22(1) because they used a legitimate, legally obtained copy of the painting; they own the device on which they reproduced the image; they did not circumvent any technological protection measures; and they kept the reproduction and used it only for private purposes.

Copyright Law and Artificial Intelligence

The development of artificial intelligence (AI) has introduced a new dimension into the question of whether a photographer holds copyright in the image.

AI refers to the simulation of human intelligence by machines performing tasks that typically require human cognitive skills such as learning, reasoning, problem-solving, perception, and language understanding. AI empowers photographers by simplifying technical tasks, expanding creative possibilities, and improving image quality, allowing them to focus more on creative vision and storytelling.

Copyright law is based on the concept of "authorship" and grants the creator of the image copyright protection.

The core issue in the dispute revolves around the level of human involvement required to qualify a work for copyright protection. Copyright law has traditionally protected works that are the result of human creativity, where the creator's personal expression, choices, and judgment are evident in the final product. However, AI systems can generate highly original works with minimal human input, often based on simple prompts or commands.

The debate, therefore, hinges on questions such as: Does using AI constitute authorship? If a human merely provides a brief prompt or instruction, is that enough to be considered a creative act deserving of copyright protection, or does copyright require more substantial involvement and personal expression?

A legal case is currently ongoing between the Samuelson-Glushko Canadian Internet Policy and Public Interest Clinic (CIPPIC) and Ankit Sahni[26] over whether artificial intelligence (AI) systems can qualify as authors under the *Copyright Act*. This dispute began when Ankit Sahni registered copyright for an image created using his AI system. CIPPIC argues that only humans can be authors, as copyright law requires human creativity and intent, which AI lacks. Sahni, however, contends that his extensive work in designing and directing AI involved enough human skill and creativity to merit copyright protection.

26 Court file number T-1717-24. The hearing of the matter is to proceed early in 2026.

The Federal Court is expected to hear the matter in the spring of 2026. The court's ruling will help clarify the extent of copyright protection for AI-generated works.

Summary

Copyright law plays a crucial role in fostering creativity and innovation by providing creators such as photographers with protection for their original work. Granting photographers the exclusive right to reproduce, distribute, and display their work is a strong incentive to produce new and exciting work.

Copyright law promotes creativity and innovation by granting photographers and other creators the exclusive rights to their original work. By providing legal protections, copyright ensures that photographers retain control over the reproduction, distribution, and public display of their images. This protection prevents unauthorized use of their work, allowing photographers to benefit financially and professionally from their efforts. In addition to acting as a safeguard against misuse, copyright protection acts as a strong motivator for photographers to explore new ideas, take creative risks, and continuously develop their artistic vision, knowing their intellectual property is safeguarded.

4

Photographing Copyrighted Material

Overview

Copyright law automatically grants photographers ownership and control over their images. However, if you photograph a painting, for example, the law balances your rights against the rights of the painting's creator. Similarly, when you photograph a person, your rights are weighed against their privacy rights. If you photograph private property, the law also considers the owner's property rights alongside yours. How does the law manage these overlapping rights? It does so by ensuring that no one's rights are unfairly infringed and requires that you obtain permission to use the photograph in certain circumstances.

Copyrighted Material

Walking through the streets of any city, you will encounter many types of copyrighted work. This includes sculptures and statues in parks, promotional posters for concerts and theatre productions displayed on walls and kiosks, and billboards and signs promoting various products and services. You might also see wall murals and graffiti created by local artists. If you are photographing these works, it is important to respect the creator's copyright interest.

How are overlapping interests of the photographer and the creator of the copyrighted material balanced? The photographer holds the rights to their creative work under the *Copyright Act*, giving them exclusive control over reproducing and distributing the image. However, the creator of the copyrighted work, such as a billboard or wall mural, also holds intellectual property rights that must be honoured. The rules the photographer is required to follow depend on how the image will be used.

Personal Use

Imagine a photographer takes a photograph of a mural on the wall of a downtown alley. The artist who created the mural holds the copyright in the mural. If the photographer is using the image solely for personal and private enjoyment, the copyright holder's permission is not needed. Private use includes such things as displaying the photograph in a home, creating a personal album, or sharing the image privately with friends and family.

Section 29.22 of the *Copyright Act* also provides an exception for private use if specific criteria are met.[1] This section permits individuals to use existing copyrighted work to create new works for non-commercial purposes without infringing the copyright.

While private use is generally safe from copyright infringement claims, photographers should be aware of the fine line between private and public use of an image. For example, sharing a photograph on social media platforms could be considered public use, potentially requiring permission from the copyright holder.

Editorial Use

If you are making someone's copyrighted work public through your photograph, you need to get the artist's consent, unless your use falls under the fair dealing provisions of the *Copyright Act*. The fair dealing provisions[2] allow for the use of copyrighted works for certain purposes without the copyright holder's permission. The uses include research, private study, education, parody or satire, criticism or review, and news reporting. These provisions are

1 *Copyright Act*, RSC 1985, c C-42, s 29.22(1).

2 Sections 29, 29.1, and 29.2 of the *Copyright Act*. For more detailed information on fair dealing provisions, you can refer to the Canadian Intellectual Property Office's Guidelines on copyright.

intended to balance the rights of the creators with the public's interest in accessing and using creative works. For example, a photograph of the mural could accompany an article about street art, urban culture, or community issues, and would fall within the news reporting category. If the photograph is used in a story that critiques the artistic style of the mural or its social message, it could fit within the criticism and review category. The photographer does not need permission from the mural's creator to use the image in this way.

The use must genuinely fit within one of the specified "fair dealing" purposes. Simply labeling a commercial use as "news reporting" or "criticism" does not automatically qualify it as fair dealing. The use must also be fair. Factors such as the purpose, character, amount, and effect of the dealing on the original work are considered. Even where a creative work falls under fair dealing provisions, giving proper credit to the original creator is necessary for criticism, review, and news reporting. If your use does not fit within these exceptions, you must obtain permission from the copyright holder to avoid infringing on their rights.

Commercial Use

Different rules apply if a photographer wants to use an image for commercial purposes. Using copyrighted material commercially without the copyright owner's permission infringes their copyright interest and could lead to a copyright infringement claim.[3] Copyright law gives the copyright holder the exclusive right to reproduce, display, and perform the work. Therefore, using the image of the street artist without permission violates their rights.

For example, suppose a photographer takes a photograph of the mural and wants to sell the photograph for use in an advertising campaign promoting tourism in the city. The artist who created the mural holds the copyright to the mural. In this case, it is not legal for the photographer to sell the image for use in the campaign without obtaining permission from the artist. The photographer must reach an agreement with the artist outlining the terms of use, any compensation the artist will receive, and how the mural will be presented in the advertising campaign. This agreement ensures that the artist's copyright interest is respected and allows the photograph to be used in the promotion legally.

Summary

Balancing the photographer's rights with the artist's rights requires careful consideration of how they overlap. The steps needed to protect the parties' interests depend on how the image will be used. If the photograph is only for private use and personal enjoyment, the photographer

3 Section 27(1) of the *Copyright Act*.

does not need permission from the artist to use it this way. If the photographer's image is used for editorial purposes, this will likely fall under the fair dealing exception, and the photographer does not need explicit permission from the artist. However, if the image is used for commercial purposes, the photographer must obtain the artist's consent.[4] Using the photograph of the mural without consent could lead to a copyright infringement action, and result in an order for damages and prohibition of further use of the image.

4 A written agreement dealing with terms of use and compensation may be required.

5
Photographing People

Overview

There are similar competing legal rights in a photograph that includes the image of an identifiable person. For the photographer who holds the copyright, the photograph is an "artistic work," just like a painting or a sculpture. The person identified in a photograph also has rights to be considered, because the photograph contains that person's "personal information."

What is the legal foundation for these rights? In *Dagg v Canada (Minister of Finance)*[1] the Supreme Court of Canada described the values underpinning privacy rights this way: "The protection of privacy is a fundamental value in modern, democratic states. . . . An expression of an individual's

1 [1997] 2 SCR 403.

unique personality or personhood, privacy is grounded on physical and moral autonomy."[2] A photograph of an identifiable person contains that person's personal information, and they have the right to control how their image is used.

Protecting Privacy Rights

Privacy rights in Canada are protected in different ways.[3] These rights are addressed in both federal and provincial legislation, and in court decisions.[4]

The federal *Personal Information Protection and Electronic Documents Act* (PIPEDA)[5] applies to private sector organizations across Canada that are engaged in commercial activity. The legislative purpose is to establish rules for how businesses collect, use, and disclose personal information in their commercial activities.[6] British Columbia,[7] Alberta,[8] and Quebec[9] have similar provincial legislation.

---

2 *Ibid* at para 65.

3 The *Canadian Charter of Rights and Freedoms,* Part I of the *Constitution Act, 1982,* being Schedule B to the *Canada Act 1982* (UK), 1982, c 11, under s 8 guarantees the right to be secure against unreasonable search and seizure, which encompasses a right to privacy. However, s 8 primarily addresses the actions of state actors.

4 For example, *Jones v Tsige* 2012 ONCA 32, 108 OR (3d) 241.

5 SC 2000, c 5.

6 Under s 4(1)(a), personal information protection requirements apply to every organization that collects, uses, or discloses personal information during its commercial activities.

7 *Personal Information Protection Act*, SBC 2003, c 63.

8 *Personal Information Protection Act*, SA 2003, c P-6.5.

9 *Act Respecting the Protection of Personal Information in the Private Sector*, CQLR c P-39.1.

In addition, the provinces of British Columbia,[10] Saskatchewan,[11] Manitoba,[12] and Newfoundland and Labrador[13] each have their own privacy legislation which focuses on protecting individuals' privacy rights which allows a statutory cause of action for the invasion of privacy.

The third source of protection is under the common law, which safeguards a reasonable expectation of privacy through principles developed by the courts. Common law torts, such as intrusion upon seclusion and public disclosure of private facts, are examples. This common law approach for defining privacy rights allows for flexibility as societal norms evolve.

Privacy is a fundamental human right that everyone possesses. It is important to understand the extent of a person's privacy rights to ensure you are complying with the law when you are photographing an identifiable person for any purpose.

PIPEDA

PIPEDA applies across all Canadian provinces and territories, and British Columbia, Alberta, and Quebec in certain circumstances. Those three provinces each have their own privacy legislation, which is like PIPEDA and applies when

10 *Privacy Act*, RSBC 1996, c 373.
11 *The Privacy Act*, RSS 1978, c P-24.
12 *The Privacy Act*, CCSM c P125.
13 *Privacy Act*, RSNL 1990, c P-22.

a business transaction takes place within the province. However, if the commercial transaction crosses a provincial or national border, PIPEDA applies to the business transaction. For example, if your photography studio is in Edmonton, Alberta, and you have a commercial contract with a client in Winnipeg, Manitoba, which involves the sharing of images of identifiable people, you need to comply with PIPEDA's privacy requirements. Determining which piece of legislation applies, federal or provincial, must be done on a case-by-case basis.

The legislative provisions in PIPEDA do not specifically mention photography. However, images that display an identifiable person fall within the definition of "personal information" under the Act.[14] As a result, businesses and organizations must obtain the consent of a person if they want to use the person's image for business purposes.[15]

Like PIPEDA, the provincial legislation in British Columbia, Alberta, and Quebec regulates the protection of personal information in private sector organizations. The provincial laws have some differences but share the common goal of protecting individuals' privacy rights when personal identifying information is being used commercially.

14 Section 2(1) of PIPEDA provides that: "personal information means information about an identifiable individual."

15 Section 2(1) of PIPEDA provides that: "commercial activity means any particular transaction, act or conduct or any regular course of conduct that is of a commercial character. . . ."

Exceptions for Journalistic, Artistic, and Literary Purposes

PIPEDA provides an exception where the image is used for journalistic, artistic, or literary purposes. The legislation does not define "journalistic purpose." However, a journalistic purpose broadly describes the gathering and dissemination of information to inform the public about events, issues, and developments, nationally and internationally.

For example, if a photojournalist captures an image of a protest in downtown Toronto and the photograph is used by a news outlet to inform the public about the event and its significance, the photojournalist will not need to get the consent of the individuals identified in the photograph. This exemption applies because the photograph serves a journalistic purpose, not a commercial purpose, by documenting and reporting on a public event.

Artists can also use images of identifiable individuals in their creations without consent, provided the purpose of the work is artistic expression or exploration. For example, a street photographer might capture candid images of people in urban settings to explore themes of city life, human emotion, or social concerns. These images can be displayed in galleries or published in books as part of the artist's body of work without requiring consent from the subjects.

In addition, a photograph can be used for literary purposes to assist with storytelling by providing context, enhancing the narrative, or illustrating themes and settings. For instance, an author might include a photograph of a bustling market scene in a book to set the stage for a chapter that takes place in that location. The image helps readers visualize the setting and understand the atmosphere, and consent from the people depicted is not required, because the photograph serves a literary purpose.

These examples highlight how images can be used in different contexts, without needing the subject's consent, if the purpose aligns with informing or enhancing public understanding and appreciation. The exemption only applies if the image of an identifiable person is used for journalistic, artistic, and literary purposes, and does not apply if it is used for any other purpose.[16]

Provincial Privacy Legislation

British Columbia, Saskatchewan, Manitoba, and Newfoundland and Labrador[17] each have their own privacy legislation that establishes a statutory tort allowing an individual to sue for damages if their privacy has been invaded.

For example, section 3(2) of the British Columbia *Privacy Act* provides that the unauthorized use of a person's portrait, still or moving, for commercial purposes is an actionable tort. Section 3(2) provides as follows:

> (2) It is a tort, actionable without proof of damage, for a person to use the name or portrait of another for the purpose of

---

16 Section 4(2)(c) provides that This Part does not apply to: "(c) any organization in respect of personal information that the organization collects, uses or discloses for journalistic, artistic or literary purposes and does not collect, use or disclose for any other purpose."

17 *Privacy Act*, RSBC 1996, c 373, s 2; *Privacy Act*, RSS 1978, c P-24; *The Privacy Act*, CCSM c P125; and *Privacy Act*, RSNL 1990, c P-22.

> advertising or promoting the sale of, or other trading in, property or services, unless that other, or a person entitled to consent on the other's behalf, consents to the use for that purpose.

Privacy rights often need to be balanced against other rights and interests. The wording of section 1 of the British Columbia *Privacy Act* is drafted to help courts apply the law in a fair and consistent manner across different cases. A violation of privacy rights is defined this way:

> (1) It is a tort, actionable without proof of damage, for a person, wilfully and without a claim of right, to violate the privacy of another.
>
> (2) The nature and degree of privacy to which a person is entitled in a situation or in relation to a matter is that which is reasonable in the circumstances, giving due regard to the lawful interests of others.
>
> (3) In determining whether the act or conduct of a person is a violation of another's privacy, regard must be given to the nature, incidence and occasion of the act or conduct and to any domestic or other relationship between the parties.

The words "without proof of damage" in section 1(1) allows individuals to bring a claim without having to prove actual harm or loss, making it easier to obtain reparation for privacy violations. The wording ensures that privacy rights are protected, even in cases where the invasion has not yet resulted in tangible harm.

The word "wilfully" in section 1(1) has been interpreted to mean "the defendant knew or ought to have known that an act would violate the privacy of the plaintiff. . . .[18] The

---

18 Report on the Privacy Act of British Columbia, 2008, British Columbia Law Institute at 11.

requirement that the violation be wilful means that accidental or unintended breaches of privacy do not result in liability, ensuring that only deliberate acts are actionable.

"Claim of right" in section 1(1) has been interpreted to mean "an honest belief in a state of facts which, if they existed, would be a legal justification or excuse."[19] The words "claim of right" were considered *St Pierre v Pacific Newspaper Group Inc*[20] where a newspaper printed a picture of the plaintiff and mislabelled him as a suspected terrorist. The person identified as the suspected terrorist was in fact a well-known lawyer who had acted for the suspected terrorist. The plaintiff alleged that his privacy had been violated. The claim for violation of privacy was dismissed because the publishers of the newspaper held an honest belief that the picture was the lawyer's client and this fell under the words, claim of right.[21]

Assume a photographer is assigned to capture lifestyle photographs for a liquor company to use in an advertisement. While walking through a residential neighbourhood, the photographer sees through the window of a house into someone's living room. They take a photograph of the interior scene without obtaining permission from the homeowner, who is inside and clearly visible. The photograph, displaying the living room and individual, is subsequently used in a liquor company's advertisement.

Despite being visible from outside, the homeowner had a reasonable expectation of privacy inside their home.

19 *Ibid.*
20 2006 BCSC 241.
21 *Ibid* at para 53.

Photographing the person through the window without their consent infringes their privacy rights.

Under section 1 of the *Privacy Act,* such an act could be considered "wilful" if the photographer knew or should have known that capturing the image intruded on the homeowner's privacy. "Wilful" in this context means that the photographer's actions were deliberate, and they were aware, or should have been aware, that their actions would violate the homeowner's privacy rights.

The photographer should have obtained permission from the homeowner before taking and using the photograph. This step is essential. If permission cannot be obtained, the photographer should not take the photograph. Adhering to privacy laws is crucial to avoid violating individuals' privacy rights and facing potential legal penalties.

In summary, a photograph of an identifiable person taken and used for commercial purposes falls within the wording of section 3(2). Using the person's image for advertising, marketing, or any other commercial activity without obtaining consent, is a violation of the person's rights under the British Columbia legislation. The privacy legislation in Saskatchewan, Manitoba, and Newfoundland and Labrador, address privacy issues in similar ways.

Common Law Privacy Rights

Under the common law, reasonable expectations of privacy are protected through common law principles developed by the courts. Courts evaluate privacy expectations on a case-by-case basis, considering factors such as the nature of the information, the context in which it was collected, and societal norms. Common law torts, such as "intrusion upon seclusion"[22] and "public disclosure of private facts,"[23] provide individuals with recourse for privacy breaches. This common law approach allows for flexibility and adaptability as societal norms and technological landscapes evolve, ensuring that privacy protections remain relevant and effective.

People enjoy privacy rights in certain locations. For example, an individual has a reasonable expectation of privacy in their home.[24] A photographer needs to obtain consent from the homeowner before taking pictures of the owner inside. By signing the consent, the owner acknowledges that they consent to being photographed and agrees to the terms set out in the agreement.

Workplaces have varying levels of privacy protection. Employees generally have a reasonable expectation of privacy in areas designated for personal use, such as break rooms, private offices, and restrooms. Photographers need to be aware of these privacy rights and obtain the necessary consent before taking photographs in the workplace to avoid infringing the employees' privacy rights.

Similarly, patients in medical facilities, such as examination rooms and treatment areas, expect their privacy to be

---

22 *Jones v Tsige* 2012 ONCA 32.

23 *Jane Doe 72511 v NM* 2018 ONSC 6607.

24 *R v Silveira* [1995] 2 SCR 297 at para 140: "There is no place on earth where persons can have a greater expectation of privacy than within their 'dwellinghouse.'"

respected. Taking photographs without permission in these settings can violate those rights. Photographers should never capture images of patients or their medical records in these areas without clear, explicit consent.[25]

Privacy Rights in a Public Place

If certain criteria are met, people enjoy privacy rights even when they are in a public place. What is a public place? Public property is property owned by the federal, provincial, territorial, and municipal governments. It includes roads, streets, sidewalks, parks, conservation areas, bicycle paths, playgrounds, city squares, and inside the public areas of buildings[26] owned by any level of government. You are permitted to take photographs anywhere on public property where there is free and unrestricted access to the public.

In *Aubry v Éditions Vice-Versa Inc*[27] the Supreme Court of Canada had to interpret Quebec's *Charter of Human Rights and Freedoms*[28] and consider the scope of privacy rights when a person is in a public place. The Supreme Court had to determine whether a woman who was photographed sitting beside a street in Montreal during a political protest had privacy rights. The woman was the central figure in the photograph, not the demonstration, and the photograph

---

25 *R v Dyment* [1988] 2 SCR 417 at para 22.
26 This is within the public area of public buildings.
27 [1998] 1 SCR 591.
28 CQLR c C-12, ss 3, 5, 9.1, and 49.

of the woman was subsequently published in a magazine without her consent.

The woman argued that taking her picture and publishing it without her consent violated her "privacy rights" under the Quebec *Charter of Human Rights and Freedoms*.[29] The Court concluded that under the Quebec *Charter* a person's right to privacy includes the person's image, the woman had a reasonable expectation of privacy in the circumstances, and the photograph should not have been published in the magazine without her consent.

It was argued that publishing the photograph in the magazine was "socially useful" and this should prevail over the woman's right to privacy. However, the Court disagreed. The Court acknowledged that while a photograph of an individual can be considered "socially useful," the social utility of the image does not override the individual's privacy rights:

> We agree with the intervener that this notion of "socially useful" refers only to the fact that the information in question has an economic, political, artistic, cultural, sporting or other value. A photograph of a single person can be "socially useful" because it serves to illustrate a theme. That does not make its publication acceptable, however, if it infringes the right to privacy.[30]

In awarding damages, the Supreme Court found that this was a commercial transaction and held that "the magazine

29 *Charter of Human Rights and Freedoms*, CQLR c C-12.
30 *Aubry v Éditions ViceVersa Inc* [1998] 1 SCR 591 at para 61.

does not cease to be 'commercial'" merely because it had an artistic content, and the photograph was used for commercial purposes to sell a magazine.[31]

In *R v Jarvis*[32] the defendant was charged under the *Criminal Code* with voyeurism[33] after he used a camera concealed inside a pen to make video recordings of female students at the high school where he was a teacher. The defendant recorded students while they were engaged in ordinary school-related activities in common areas of the school, including classrooms and hallways. Most of the videos focused on the faces and upper bodies of female students. The students did not know they were being photographed.[34]

The Supreme Court of Canada held that a court must consider the entire context in which the observation or recording took place. To make that determination, considerations may include the location, the nature of the conduct, whether it consisted of observation or recording, the awareness or the consent of the person who was recorded, the relationship between the parties, and the way the recording was done.[35] What the Supreme Court was saying was that privacy is not an "all-or-nothing" concept. In other words, simply because a person is in circumstances where they do

31 *Ibid* at para 74.

32 [2019] 1 SCR 488.

33 Section 162 of the *Criminal Code*, RSC 1985, c C-46, makes it an offence to surreptitiously observe or make a visual recording of a person who is in circumstances that give rise to a reasonable expectation of privacy.

34 *R v Jarvis* [2019] 1 SCR 488 at para 2.

35 *Ibid* at para 5.

not expect complete privacy does not mean that they waive all reasonable expectations of privacy.[36]

The Court's second point focused on the distinction between simply observing a person and recording their image with a camera. The Court noted that intrusion on privacy is fundamentally different when a person makes a visual recording:

> A visual recording may be able to capture a level of detail that the human eye cannot. A visual recording can also capture this detail in a permanent form that can be accessed, edited, manipulated and studied.[37]

In other words, taking a photograph of a person intrudes on their privacy right, more than just observing them.

In summary, the *Aubry* case establishes that even in public spaces, individuals may have a right to privacy, and this includes their image. It can be argued that the reasoning in *Aubry* does not apply to the common law jurisdiction in Canada because it involved the interpretation of Quebec's legislation. However, given the importance of privacy rights as defined by the Supreme Court, lower courts in common law jurisdictions are likely to consider similar factors when determining whether a reasonable expectation of privacy exists. In *R v Jarvis*, the Court emphasized that privacy is context-dependent and not an all-or-nothing concept. The Court also ruled that taking a photograph is more invasive than simply observing a person.

36 *Ibid* at para 61.
37 *Ibid* at para 62.

Before taking a photograph, photographers should assess the context to determine whether capturing the image might be considered intrusive or a violation of privacy. This includes considering the location, the nature of the activity, and the potential use of the image. Photographers should also seek explicit consent when photographing individuals, particularly in situations where privacy could be expected, or when the images will be used for publication or commercial purposes.

An Identifiable Person

What makes a person identifiable?[38] Recognition can arise through different means, not just a person's face. If the face is not fully visible, there may be other features that can make a person identifiable. This can include unique tattoos, birthmarks or scars, or distinctive clothes. Sometimes the context in which the person is photographed can identify a person, such as the activity for which the person is famous. For example, a photograph showing only the back of a professional hockey player wearing an Edmonton Oilers sweater with number 99 would identify Wayne Gretzky.

38 In *Gordon v Canada (Health)* 2008 FC 258 at para 34, the Federal Court adopted the following test: "[The i]nformation will be about an identifiable individual where there is a serious possibility that an individual could be identified through the use of that information, alone or in combination with other available information."

Obtaining Consent

It is important to maintain an ethical approach when you obtain a person's consent to use their image. There should be open communication in which you explain the purpose of the photographs, how the person's image will be used, and any potential implications. Be alert to cultural considerations that may have an impact on the person's decision and provide the person with any information they need to make an informed decision. Acknowledge the person's right to control their image and make the decision about how it will be used. Ensure they know they have the right to say no.

Sometimes if the person is still uncertain about whether to consent to the use of their image, you can offer other options. For example, if the person does not want their image posted on a public site like Facebook or Instagram, they may be agreeable to having it used for a social cause they care about, or for some other purpose that interests them.

Personal Use

Using a photograph of an identifiable person strictly for private purposes generally eliminates any legal concerns. Since the image is not shared publicly or used for commercial gain, it does not infringe on the individual's privacy rights or violate copyright laws. Examples of private use might include displaying the photograph in a home, using the photograph in a personal memory book, or using a photograph as a screensaver on a personal device. Personal use respects the person's privacy and does not exploit the image in any way through public sharing or for financial gain. You are unlikely to run into any legal problems if your photograph of an identifiable individual is only for private use.

Editorial Use

When considering uploading a photograph of an identifiable person to a social media site like Facebook or for publication in a magazine, it is important to consider whether consent is required. Posting an image of an identifiable person on an editorial site holds the potential for wide distribution of a person's image, making it available to thousands of people.

While there is no legislation requiring a person's consent before a photograph containing a person's image is shared for editorial purposes, it is wise to obtain the person's consent. In *Aubry* the Supreme Court found that an image can be "socially useful," as in the editorial context, but it still infringes a person's right to privacy. Obtaining a person's consent before you post their image on an editorial site[39] shows respect for the person's privacy rights and allows the person to make an informed decision about whether they

39 Editorial use is where the photograph is shared publicly in news articles, magazines, blogs, or other media outlets to inform, educate, or comment on a newsworthy event, topic, or issue, and on social media sites such as Facebook.

want their image shared at all.[40] People sometimes have cultural or religious reasons for not wanting to have their image made public.

Seeking permission should include explaining how you intend to use the photograph, and where you intend to post it. Asking for the person's consent allows the person to raise any concerns and satisfy themselves that the image is not harmful, embarrassing, or offensive in some way. Verbal permission is an option but written permission by way of release is the best approach if you want to create a record of what you have done.

Commercial Use

In Canada, using someone's image for commercial purposes requires their consent due to privacy protections under federal and provincial legislation. PIPEDA and similar provincial laws in British Columbia, Alberta, and Quebec mandate that businesses obtain consent before using identifiable images for commercial purposes. Additionally, privacy legislation in British Columbia, Saskatchewan, Manitoba, and Newfoundland and Labrador, create statutory torts that allow individuals to sue if their image is used commercially without their consent. Failing to obtain consent in these situations can have serious consequences, resulting in lawsuits and damages. Therefore, it is essential to ensure you have permission before using someone's image commercially.

---

40 *Aubry v Éditions Vice-Versa Inc* [1998] 1 SCR 591.

Summary

Protecting privacy rights is essential in photography, as it balances the rights of the photographer with those of individuals whose images are captured. While photographers hold copyright over their work as an "artistic creation," the people depicted also possess significant rights related to their personal information. Canadian privacy laws, including the *Personal Information Protection and Electronic Documents Act* (PIPEDA) and various provincial statutes, enforce these protections, especially when images are used for commercial purposes. Court decisions in Canada have reinforced the importance of privacy rights, underscoring that individuals are entitled to a reasonable expectation of privacy even in certain public or semi-public contexts. Photographers are encouraged to adopt ethical practices by obtaining explicit consent, especially when capturing images of identifiable people in contexts where privacy might be reasonably expected.

6
Property Rights

Overview

The third area where a photographer's interests can overlap with those of a third party's is when you photograph private property. A property interest exists in a wide range of buildings, including office buildings and factories, private residences, and religious sites, such as temples, churches, mosques, and synagogues. What are the respective rights of the photographer and the property owner if, for example, you photograph a building, or some other type of private property? Again, there are competing legal rights[1] that exist in an image displaying property.

1 The competing interests are similar to when you take photographs of identifiable individuals.

The photographer owns the copyright in the photograph of the property, but the property owner has the right to control how the property is depicted. Canadian common law supports the rights of property owners to control activities on their property, such as photography. In addition, Ontario's *Trespass to Property Act*[2] gives property owners the right to control access and activities on their property, including photography.

In Canada, the level of control the property owner can assert depends in part on where the photograph is taken. When a photograph is taken from a public location, such as a street or sidewalk, the property owner does not have the same level of control as when a photograph is taken on the property itself.

Differences Between Public Locations and Private Property

Whether you are taking a photograph of a building from a public location, or on the property itself, there are certain causes of action that are common to both. These include defamation, implied endorsement, and trademark infringement. Claims of this kind can arise regardless of the spot from which the photograph is taken because they are tied to the use of the images, rather than the location the photograph was taken.

---

2 RSO 1990, c T.21, s 2(1).

Personal Use

When you take a photograph of a building from a public location, such as a street or sidewalk, privacy rights are not an issue. This is because there is no reasonable expectation of privacy for anything visible from a public place. Copyright rules do not allow the owner to control how the property is depicted in an image.[3] Similarly, trespassing issues do not arise because the photograph is taken from a public location. If the building features visible trademarks, such as logos or brand names, this does not raise legal concerns. In other words, photographs taken for personal use do not present a problem.

When the photograph is being taken on the property itself, you need explicit permission from the property owner to access and photograph a building on private property. Without the owner's consent, entering and photographing the property can lead to a trespassing claim. There is also a higher expectation of privacy on private property, and photographers must ensure they do not capture sensitive or private information that violates the privacy rights of the property owner or someone else on the property.

Editorial Use

While property owners have certain rights, these do not typically extend to controlling the depiction of their property for editorial use when the photograph is taken from a

---

3 Section 32.2(1)(b) of the Canadian *Copyright Act*, RSC 1985, c C-42, provides that it is not an infringement of copyright to take a photograph of an architectural work, if it is permanently situated in a public place.

public space. For instance, a photograph taken from a public sidewalk showing an office tower can be used in a newspaper article discussing urban development or architectural styles, without the consent of the property owner.

Taking photographs on private property for editorial purposes requires explicit permission from the property owner. Unauthorized access can also result in trespassing claims against the photographer. Photographers must ensure they do not capture private information or misrepresent the property in some way. The heightened expectation of privacy on private property necessitates careful consideration of what is photographed and how it is used.

Commercial Use

Additional legal considerations can arise when photographing a building for commercial purposes, whether the photograph is taken from a public space or on the property itself. As a photographer, you need to avoid doing anything that could result in a claim for trademark infringement, implied endorsement, or defamation.

Trademark Infringement and Implied Endorsement

How is trademark infringement different from implied endorsement? Suppose a photographer is hired by a local clothing brand in Vancouver to create a series of advertisements for their new line of luxury outerwear. The photographer decides to photograph the model in front of a famous building in Toronto, the "Maple Tower," which is known for its distinctive architecture and is owned by a high-end real estate company called "Maple Realty." The Maple Realty logo, which is a registered trademark, is prominently displayed on the building's facade.

Trademark Infringement

In one of the photographs, the Maple Realty logo is clearly visible on the building in the background, positioned in such a way that it appears to be part of the clothing brand's advertisement. When the photographs are published, Maple Realty notices that the public is beginning to associate their brand with the clothing line, with some customers even calling to ask if Maple Realty has launched a new clothing venture. In this scenario, trademark infringement could be claimed by Maple Realty because the use of their logo in the advertisement is causing confusion among consumers, leading them to believe that Maple Realty is connected to or endorses the clothing brand. The key issue is that the use of the logo has created a likelihood of confusion about the source or sponsorship of the goods.

Implied Endorsement

In a separate version of the advertisement, the photographer decides to edit the photographs to make the Maple Realty logo more prominent and places the clothing brand's tagline right next to it, giving the impression that Maple Realty is endorsing the clothing line. The tagline reads, "Worn by those who live the Maple lifestyle," subtly suggesting that Maple Realty's clients, known for their luxury tastes, prefer this brand of outerwear. Even if there is no actual confusion about who is selling the clothing, implied endorsement could be claimed by Maple Realty. They could argue that the advertisement falsely implies that Maple Realty endorses or supports the clothing line, potentially leading to harm to their brand, to promote a product with which they have no connection.

What are the key distinctions? With trademark infringement the issue is consumer confusion. The public might mistakenly believe that Maple Realty is involved in the production or is the source of the clothes. Implied endorsement, on the other hand, suggests a false association or approval by Maple Realty, without consumer confusion about the source.

In summary, the photographer's decision to include the Maple Realty logo in the advertisement without permission opens the door to legal challenges on both fronts. Whether it's trademark infringement due to consumer confusion or implied endorsement suggesting a false connection, both situations pose significant legal risks to the photographer.

Defamation

When using a photograph of a building for commercial purposes, it is also important not to misrepresent the property or its owner in a way that is defamatory. Defamation occurs when false information is published that harms someone's reputation. To avoid defamation, it is crucial that the image and any accompanying text accurately represent the property and does not contain misleading or incorrect information.

For example, if a photograph of a well-maintained office building was used in an advertisement for a real estate company that implies the building is outdated or in need of significant repairs, to promote a competing property, this could damage the property owner's reputation. The advertisement should only include accurate, factual, and verifiable information about the state of the property. Ensuring accurate representation helps protect the property owner's reputation and avoids potential legal issues related to defamation.

While the primary responsibility for preventing defamation typically lies with the publisher or client using the photograph, the photographer should take proactive steps to protect against defamation risks, including discussing the intended use of the photograph with clients.

Photographs Taken on the Property

To use a photograph taken on private property for commercial purposes, you need to obtain explicit permission in the form of a property release from the property owner. A property release is a legal document that states how the photographs can be used, for how long, and in what context. A release helps prevent misunderstandings and ensures both parties agree on the terms of use.

If you enter private property and take photographs without permission, you could face a trespassing claim. Photographers must also be careful not to capture private information as there is a higher expectation of privacy on private property. For example, when taking photographs, avoid including visible documents, computer screens, or personal items that reveal private information.

Areas not visible from public spaces, like backyards, interiors, or private gatherings, should be treated with extra care because the property owner expects these spaces to remain private. Taking pictures of individuals without their consent can lead to privacy violations. Even if you are focusing on the building, avoid including identifiable individuals in the background unless they have given their consent.

Summary

The main differences between photographing public and private sites for commercial use are as follows: (1) On private property, you need explicit permission and a property release from the owner. This document specifies how the photographs can be used and helps prevent misunderstandings; (2) Private properties have a higher expectation of privacy. You must be more careful about what you photograph and how the images are used; (3) Unauthorized entry and photography on private property can lead to a trespassing claim; and (4) You have a greater responsibility to avoid capturing private information and infringing on people's privacy rights. Areas like backyards, interiors, or private gatherings require extra care.

In public spaces you generally have more freedom to take and use photographs for commercial purposes. However, you must still avoid infringing on trademarks, creating implied endorsements, or inaccurately representing the property and its owner. Even though public spaces have a lower expectation of privacy, capturing identifiable individuals without their consent in some cases can still lead to privacy claims.

Other Types of Property

A property interest exists in a wide range of things including cars, boats, and aircraft, and even identifiable animals.

Suppose that a professional photographer spots a vintage sports car parked in a public space during a car show and takes several photographs of the car, and they plan to use these photographs for private, editorial, and commercial purposes.

Private Use

If the photographer takes a picture of the sports car for personal use, they generally have no legal worries where the car is photographed in a public space. Personal use includes adding the photograph to a private album, using it as a screensaver, or displaying it at home. Since the image is not being distributed or used commercially, the car owner's rights are not affected, and no permission is needed.

Editorial Use

If the car is photographed in a public space, the car owner has limited control over its use for editorial purposes since there is no expectation of privacy in public areas. The photographer typically does not need permission to include the photograph in a news article about vintage car shows, an automotive blog, or a magazine feature on classic cars. However, it is crucial that the photograph and accompanying content accurately represent the car and its context. Misleading or false representations that could harm the car owner's reputation might lead to a defamation claim.

Commercial Use

First, the photographer should obtain a release from the owner of the the sports car granting them permission to use the photograph commercially. The release should outline the terms of use, including any limitation on how the image can be used and whether compensation is required.

Next, you need to ensure that the image does not infringe on any intellectual property rights, such as trademarks, or copyrighted designs associated with the car. The name of the sports car and any logos or other identifying marks are likely registered trademarks owned by the company. These distinguishing trademarks will be protected under trademark law. The design elements of the sports car, including its body shape, exterior features, and interior design may also be subject to copyright protection if they meet the originality threshold required under copyright law. The company may also have specific policies regarding the use of its trademarks and vehicle designs in commercial photography situations. You will need to contact the department in the company that deals with trademarks and brand management to provide guidance on the necessary steps to obtain a licence allowing you to sell your image commercially.

In summary, managing the dynamics between the rights of the photographer who holds the copyright, and the parties that also have an interest in the image as property owners, demands an understanding of both intellectual property and property rights. It is crucial to ensure the image is used in a way that complies with the law.

7

Licensing Your Photographs

Overview

A licensing agreement is an agreement between the licensor, who hold the copyright in the photograph, and the licensee who want to use the image. As the creator and owner of the image, the licensor has the sole right to decide how the image is used. The agreement is a contract that outlines the terms for using the image, such as the length of time it can used, where it can be used, and how much the licensee must pay.

Special Types of Licences

There are different types of licensing arrangements: exclusive and non-exclusive licences, rights-managed licences, and royalty-free licences.

Exclusive and Non-exclusive Licences

In an exclusive licence agreement, only one person or business, known as the licensee, can use the image. The licensor, who is the copyright holder, agrees not to allow anyone else to use the image during the term of the agreement. This arrangement gives the licensee a competitive advantage in certain situations. For the copyright holder, an exclusive licence means having complete control over how the photograph is used. Typically, exclusive licences come with higher fees because only one licensee has the right to use the image. However, there are drawbacks. Since only one licensee can use the photograph, it may not get as much exposure and may not be seen by as many people. Additionally, if the licensee encounters business problems, it could have an impact on the revenue stream.

Conversely, a non-exclusive licence allows the copyright holder to grant permission to multiple people or businesses to use the image. Several licensees can use the same photograph for the same or different purposes as outlined in their licences. The main advantage of a non-exclusive licence is wider distribution of the image, which increases the exposure and revenue. It also reduces financial risk because income is not reliant on a single licensee. However, if multiple licensees use the photograph at the same time, its value might decrease because it can become overused and lose its uniqueness.

Rights-Managed Licences

In a rights-managed licence, the details about how the photograph can be used are more specific than other types of licences. These agreements outline where, how, and for what purposes the photograph can be used. For example, the licence might specify that the photograph can only appear in a particular magazine issue, on a specific website, or within certain geographic boundaries. A rights-managed licence defines the permitted uses of the photograph, including its size, placement, duration of use, and distribution. The negotiation process allows for tailoring the agreement to meet the needs of both the licensor and licensee. These agreements can include provisions for digital tracking and monitoring, such as digital watermarks or unique identifiers, to ensure compliance with the terms of the agreement.

There are benefits to a rights-managed licence. It offers flexibility and customization, allowing the copyright holder to control how and where the photograph is used, tailored to specific markets and regions. The parties can negotiate terms that suit their needs. This customized approach ensures both parties get what they want, but it often comes at a higher cost due to the specialized nature of the agreement.

However, there are also drawbacks. Customizing the agreement can be more complex and time-consuming compared to other types of licences. The restrictions on usage terms, such as specifying where and how the photograph can be used, can pose challenges for the licensee by limiting the flexibility in usage.

Royalty-Free Licences

A royalty-free licence allows the licensee to use the image without paying royalties each time it is used. Instead, the licensee pays a one-time fee upfront to obtain the licence, which grants broad rights to use the image. This type of licence is cost-effective for the licensee, providing access to high-quality images without the need for ongoing negotiations or payments for each use. This can save both time and money, especially for businesses or individuals who need to use the image multiple times or across different media.

However, there is a downside to royalty-free licences: the lack of exclusivity. Since royalty-free licences are non-exclusive, multiple licensees can use the same photograph simultaneously. This may reduce the photograph's uniqueness for certain purposes. From the copyright holder's perspective, there is also less control over how the photograph is used once it is licensed royalty-free. Licensees can use the image in ways the photographer did not anticipate. This type of licensing is common on stock photography websites.

Licensing Agreement Provisions to Consider

A licensing agreement should address several key issues. When creating a licence, it is important to clearly define the rights being granted. Detailing these points helps avoid confusion and ensures both parties understand the agreement.

Copyright Ownership

The agreement should state that the photographer keeps ownership of the copyright and that the licence is limited to the rights described in the agreement. It should also specify if the licensee can sublicense the image or is the photographer's permission is needed first.

Payments and Royalties

Compensation under a licensing agreement can be managed in different ways. The licensor might request a one-time fee when the agreement is signed. If the image generates sales revenue, the licensee may be required to pay royalties. It is important to decide how often payments will be made and how they will be structured. The licensor can ask for the right to audit the licensee's financial records to ensure accuracy. Taxes are another consideration. The licensee can agree to withhold taxes and send them to the tax authority. The method of payment, such as electronic transfer, should also be agreed upon. Late payment penalties are sometimes imposed. Clearly detailing these aspects helps both parties understand their financial responsibilities.

Credit and Attribution

The agreement should state whether the licensee must give credit to the photographer when using the photograph. If credit is required, the agreement should specify where the credit will be placed and in what format.[1] As a photographer, you will likely want credit because it helps build your reputation and business. This part of the agreement can also

---

1 The "format" refers to the detailed specifications about how the photographer's credit should appear.

include the relief you are entitled to if the licensee fails to provide proper credit.

Representations and Warranties

Both parties should confirm that they have the right and authority to enter into the agreement and fulfill their obligations. The licensee needs to be sure that the photographer owns the photograph and has the right to license it without infringing on any third-party rights. This means the photograph's use does not violate the rights of third parties who are not part of the licensing agreement.

Infringing third-party rights can happen in different ways. The agreement should confirm that the licensor has not infringed any third parties' copyrights or trademarks. The licensee will also want assurance that no third parties' privacy or publicity rights have been violated. Additionally, the licensor must ensure that the photograph does not violate the property rights of a third party. When a photograph depicts private property without obtaining the proper permissions or releases, it can infringe on the rights of the property owner. Private property includes any property owned by individuals or companies, such as buildings, homes, land, or personal belongings.

Indemnity and Liability

The agreement should specify whether the licensor or licensee is responsible for any claims, damages, or liabilities that come from using the photograph. This includes issues like copyright infringement, defamation, or privacy rights violations. The photographer might agree to protect the licensee against claims resulting from the photographer's breach of any representations or warranties. Similarly, the licensee can agree to indemnify the photographer against claims resulting from the licensee's breach of representations or warranties, or from unauthorized use of the photographs.

The agreement usually requires the indemnified party to promptly notify the indemnifying party of any claim for which indemnification is sought. Additionally, there may be a clause requiring both parties to maintain appropriate insurance coverage for any indemnification obligations under the agreement.

Termination and Breach

The agreement should outline the conditions under which either party can terminate the licensing agreement. Common grounds for termination include the following: (1) If one party fundamentally breaches the contract, the other party has the right to terminate the agreement. A fundamental breach could include serious violations such as unauthorized use of the photograph or failure to adhere to the agreed-upon terms and conditions; (2) If the licensee fails to make the required payments, the licensor can terminate the agreement. This ensures that the licensor is compensated as agreed to; (3) If both parties can agree to terminate the contract at any time, this mutual termination provision should be documented to avoid future disputes; and (4) The agreement should also include a clause detailing the procedures for dispute resolution to address any conflicts that arise. This would typically involve options such as negotiations, mediation, and arbitration.

Governing Law and Jurisdiction

The parties should agree on the jurisdiction and the law that will govern the interpretation of the licensing agreement. If the licensing agreement is with a party outside of Canada, you should consider a few factors when choosing the governing law: will the copyright laws in that jurisdiction adequately protect the parties' interests? Will the damages awarded in the chosen jurisdiction be enforceable? Does the jurisdiction have the necessary expertise to handle the dispute? Are there benefits such as efficiency or reasonable costs if the dispute is resolved in that jurisdiction? Is the chosen jurisdiction convenient for all parties? Choosing the right jurisdiction helps ensure that the agreement is interpreted fairly and that any legal disputes are resolved effectively.

Registering Licensing Agreement

In Canada you should register the licensing agreement with the Canadian Intellectual Property Office (CIPO). There are benefits to registration in Canada as well as internationally.

Registering the agreement with the CIPO establishes a public record which is helpful in proving ownership of the copyright if a dispute arises. Copyright registration creates a presumption of validity for copyright works. Section 34.1(1) of the *Copyright Act*[2] provides that:

> 34.1 (1) In any civil proceedings taken under this Act in which the defendant puts in issue either the existence of the copyright or the title of the plaintiff to it,
>
> (a) copyright shall be presumed, unless the contrary is proved, to subsist in the work, performer's performance, sound recording or communication signal, as the case may be; and
>
> (b) the author, performer, maker or broadcaster, as the case may be, shall, unless the contrary is proved, be presumed to be the owner of the copyright.

In other words, the registration certificate creates a legal presumption of both copyright's existence and ownership, unless there is evidence to the contrary.

Registration can also facilitate international protection through treaties that Canada has signed. The Berne Convention for the Protection of Literary and Artistic Works,[3] which Canada is a signatory to, plays an important role. While registering a licensing agreement with CIPO is not a requirement for international protection under the Berne Convention there are advantages, nonetheless. Having a registered licensing agreement and the associated copyright registration can simplify enforcing the right in a foreign jurisdiction, by providing clear evidence of the copyright owner's rights.

---

2 RSC 1985, c C-42.

3 The Berne Convention for the Protection of Literary and Artistic Works, 9 September 1886, as revised at Paris on 24 July 1971, and amended on 28 September 1979.

Creative Commons Licensing

If you are more interested in getting exposure for your work than generating revenue, you should consider posting your photographs on Creative Commons.[4] Creative Commons, founded in 2001, is a non-profit organization that is dedicated to the distribution of copyrighted work under a licensing system that allows for the sharing of your work on terms not as strict as the conventional licensing arrangement. The organization provides free standardized licences that photographers can use to grant other parties permission to use their images while retaining their copyright interest in their images. These licences offer various options, letting photographers decide how much freedom to give to the licensee. On the restrictive end, licences require attribution and prohibit commercial use. On the permissive end, licences allow commercial use and derivative works without restrictions. A derivative work is a new creation derived from the original image, such as a collage or montage.

There are five different types of licences:

1. Attribution (CC BY)
   This licence offers the most freedom, allowing others to distribute, remix, adapt, and build upon the creator's work, including for commercial purposes. The only requirement is that appropriate credit must be given to the original creator.

---

4 Creative Commons, 171 Second Street, Suite 300, San Francisco, CA 94105, USA, online: https://creativecommons.org.

2. Attribution-ShareAlike (CC BY-SA)
   This licence allows others to remix, adapt, and build upon the creator's work, including for commercial purposes, if they credit the original creator. Any new creations that incorporate the original work must be licensed under the same terms as the original licence, ensuring that derivative works remain freely available under the same conditions.
3. Attribution-NoDerivatives (CC BY-ND)
   This licence permits others to redistribute the work, including commercially, but it cannot be altered or transformed in any way. The original creator must be credited, and the work must be passed along unchanged.
4. Attribution-NonCommercial-ShareAlike (CC BY-NC-SA)
   This licence lets others remix, adapt, and build upon the work, but only for non-commercial purposes. Credit must be given to the original creator, and any derivative works must be licensed under identical terms, ensuring that all future works remain non-commercial and freely available under the same conditions.
5. Attribution-NonCommercial-NoDerivatives (CC BY-NC-ND)
   This is the most restrictive licence, allowing others to download and share the work, but it cannot be used commercially, modified, or built upon in any way. The original creator must be credited, and the work must be used exactly as is, without any alterations or commercial use.

Creative commons licences are designed to provide creators with different ways to share their work with others, while at the same time maintaining their copyright interest in the images they share.

Benefits of Licensing Your Photograph

In summary, licensing your photograph has several advantages: licensing allows you to earn money from your work by charging a fee for its use. Depending on the agreement, you can receive royalties each time your photograph is used. This can create a steady income stream, especially if your photograph is in high demand.

You have control over how your image is used. You can specify where and for how long your photograph can be used, ensuring it aligns with your preferences and values. This control helps maintain the integrity of your work and prevents it from being used in ways of which you do not approve.

Licensing can also significantly boost your visibility and reputation as a photographer. When your work is used in various media and by reputable organizations, it helps your portfolio reach a broader audience. This increased exposure can enhance your reputation and attract more clients or commissions.

Licensing your photograph through a well-drafted agreement offers significant benefits. It defines the terms of use, ensuring that your work is properly credited and protected against unauthorized usage, while also providing avenues for recourse if your photographs are misused.

Overall, a strong licensing agreement ensures your photographic work is used according to your terms.

8

Assigning Your Copyright Interest

Overview

When you license your copyright interest in the photograph, you retain ownership of the copyright, but you grant the licensee permission to use the copyrighted image on certain conditions. When you assign your copyright interest, you are transferring all or part of the copyright ownership to another party. Section 13(4) of the *Copyright Act*[1] provides that:

> (4) The owner of the copyright in any work may assign the right, either wholly or partially, and either generally or subject to limitations relating to territory, medium or sector of the market or other limitations relating to the scope of the assignment,

1 RSC 1985, c C-42.

> and either for the whole term of the copyright or for any other part thereof, and may grant any interest in the right by licence, but no assignment or grant is valid unless it is in writing signed by the owner of the right in respect of which the assignment or grant is made, or by the owner's duly authorized agent.

Section 13(4) offers a great deal of flexibility in how copyright ownership can be transferred. The section provides for transfer of the copyright either "wholly or partially." An "assignment" of copyright is a complete transfer of ownership rights, and the copyright owner relinquishes all control, whereas a "grant" of copyright is a partial transfer of rights. For example, a photographer can transfer the entire copyright in a photograph, or only the right to display the photograph on social media sites, while retaining all other rights. For the assignment to be valid, the assignment or grant must be signed by the copyright owner or an authorized agent.

It is wise to register the change in ownership with the Copyright Office of the Canadian Intellectual Property Office (CIPO).[2] This protects your legal rights and permits you to bring legal proceedings against anyone who may be using your copyright without your consent. Registration involves preparation of the necessary documents, completion of the online application, uploading the necessary supporting documents, and paying the required fee. After

2 For general inquiries and assistance you can reach CIPO's Client Service Centre, online: cipo.contact@canada.ca. The CIPO website also has helpful resources, online: https://ised-isde.canada.ca/site/canadian-intellectual-property-office/en.

receiving and processing the application CIPO issues a certificate of registration confirming the change of ownership in the assignment.

Advantages and Disadvantages of Assignment

As with most things, there are advantages and disadvantages to consider. The advantage of a full assignment of copyright is that it frees you from control and responsibility for the copyrighted work. When you assign your copyright, it usually involves a lump sum payment, which can provide immediate financial rewards for your work. This can be particularly beneficial if you need quick access to funds or if you prefer a one-time payment over potentially uncertain future earnings.

However, there are also drawbacks. With the assignment of your interest, you no longer have any control over how the image is used or distributed. You also forego any potential revenues or royalties that the photograph might have generated in the future. This means you miss out on any long-term financial benefits that could arise from the ongoing use of your work.

Additionally, there is the possibility that the assignee will use your image in ways of which you do not approve. They might alter the image, use it in a context you find inappropriate, or associate it with products, services, or ideas that conflict with your values. While you retain moral rights to your work, which provide a way to address certain types of concerns, they do not give you complete control. Moral rights allow you to object to uses that would harm your reputation or integrity as the creator. However, once the copyright is assigned, your legal ability to influence or restrict the assignee's use of the image is limited to the protection moral rights provide.

Assignment Agreement Clauses

An assignment agreement should address several issues, many of which are like those in a licensing agreement. The primary purpose is to transfer copyright ownership from one party to another, ensuring all legal matters are covered to avoid future disputes.

Identification of Parties

This section identifies the parties involved in the agreement, clearly stating who the current copyright owner (assignor) is and who the recipient (assignee) will be. Clear identification ensures the agreement is enforceable against the correct parties and that there is no ambiguity about who holds the rights to the photographs.

Description of Photographs

A clear and detailed description of the photographs being assigned is crucial. This section should include titles, dates, file names, and any other relevant identifying information. A precise description prevents any uncertainty regarding which photographs are covered by the agreement, ensuring both parties have a mutual understanding of the assignment's scope.

Transfer of Copyright Ownership

This core provision establishes the legal basis for the assignment. It outlines that the assignor is transferring all rights, title, and interest in the copyright of the identified photographs to the assignee. This section legally formalizes the transfer of ownership, ensuring that the assignee gains all the rights previously held by the assignor. It is important to clearly state the extent of the rights being transferred to avoid any future disputes.

Consideration

This paragraph details the consideration, or payment, to be made by the assignee to the assignor for the photographs. It should specify the amount, method, and terms of payment. Clear terms regarding consideration help avoid disputes over payment and ensure that both parties agree on the value of the transferred rights. Properly defining the financial aspects of the agreement helps ensure transparency and fairness in the transaction.

Representation and Warranties

There are certain common representations and warranties that should be included in assignment agreements. The assignor should be prepared to represent and warrant that: (1) they are the sole and exclusive owner of the copyright in the photographs and has the legal right to transfer the copyright to the assignee; (2) the copyright in the photographs is valid and enforceable, and there are no challenges to the copyright's validity; (3) the photographs do not infringe upon the intellectual property rights of any third party; (4) they have full legal authority to enter into the assignment agreement and to transfer the copyright in the photographs; (5) they have not previously assigned, licensed, or transferred copyright in the photographs to any other party; and (6) all the information provided to the assignee, including descriptions of the photographs, is accurate and complete.

These representations and warranties provide assurances to the assignee that the assignor has the right to transfer the copyright and that there are no undisclosed issues with the photographs.

Indemnification

The indemnification section ensures that the assignor agrees to indemnify the assignee against any claims, damages, or liabilities that arise from the assignment. This provision protects the assignee from potential legal issues that might arise due to past actions or claims related to the photographs, ensuring the assignee is not held liable for issues originating during the assignor's time as the copyright holder. Indemnification clauses are essential to protect the assignee's interests, and offer a clear solution if issues arise.

In summary, clear terms addressing these key areas helps ensure a smooth transfer of copyright ownership and protects both parties.

9

Releases

Obtaining a Release

A release is a legal agreement that grants permission from the identifiable person or property owner (the releasor) to the photographer (releasee), allowing for the use of the person's image or the property's image, on specified terms. Obtaining a release for images of property and people is essential for legal and ethical reasons. For property, a release ensures that the photographer has permission to use images of recognizable property, protecting against potential claims of unauthorized use. By signing a release, a person agrees to let their image be used, reducing the risk of future legal problems and ensuring everyone's rights are protected.

Property Rights

Owners of private property, such as buildings, have control over how their property is depicted and used in photographs. While the property itself is not protected by copyright, the owner can still control how it is used in photographs, especially for commercial purposes. A property release grants permission from the owner, allowing you to use the photograph legally for things like advertisements or products.

Privacy Rights

If the photograph of an identifiable person is only for the photographer's personal use and not shared publicly or commercially, a release is not required.

If the photograph of an identifiable person is used for editorial purposes, such as news reporting, commentary, or educational content, a release is also typically not required. However, this depends on context, and privacy laws in certain jurisdictions may still apply if the use invades the person's reasonable expectation of privacy. Always review specific provincial laws.

A release is required when a person's identifiable image is used for commercial purposes to protect their privacy and control over how their likeness is exploited. This protection ensures that individuals have control over whether their image can be used, and how it will be used to promote a product, service, or brand.

Right of Publicity

The right of publicity is a legal right that allows individuals to control and profit from the commercial use of their name, image, or likeness. This prevents unauthorized commercial exploitation and ensures they are compensated for the use of their image. Obtaining a release form allows photographers and businesses to legally use a person's image in advertisements, marketing, and other commercial activities, protecting them from potential lawsuits. This process respects the individual's rights, and ensures their image is used appropriately in a commercial context.

Terms Ordinarily Used in a Release

Identification of Parties

The identification of parties in a release names the person granting the release (the releasor) and the person receiving it (the releasee). This section ensures there is no ambiguity about who is involved in the agreement. Clearly identifying the parties helps ensure that the agreement is enforceable and that both parties understand who holds the rights to the property or material in question.

Description of Image

The description of the image clause provides a detailed account of the specific image being covered. For example, it might state, "The Releasor grants the Releasee the right to use the photograph titled 'Sunset Over Lake Huron taken on June 5, 2022.'" This clause includes details such as titles, dates, and file names to ensure both parties understand which image is being referenced. By doing so, it avoids any confusion or disputes about the scope of the release and ensures that the agreed-upon image is used according to the terms specified.

Scope of Use

The scope of use clause in a release agreement specifies how the released property, such as a photograph, can be used. This clause sets clear boundaries to prevent misuse by defining the permitted uses, duration, and geographic limitations. For instance, it might state, "The Releasee may use the photograph for commercial advertising, including print and digital media, worldwide for three years." By specifying these details, the clause makes sure the property or material is used according to the agreed terms, offering legal protection and clarity for both parties involved

Consideration

The consideration clause details the payment or benefit exchanged for granting the release, ensuring the agreement is legally binding by demonstrating that something of value is being exchanged. For example, "In consideration for this release, the Releasor will receive a payment of

$500." By clearly stating the amount, method, and terms of payment, this clause helps avoid disputes and ensures both parties understand and agree on the value of the rights being transferred. Clarity strengthens the enforceability of the contract.

Waiver of Rights

The waiver of rights clause in a release agreement ensures that the releasor gives up any future claims to additional compensation or control over the released material. This guarantees the releasee full and undisputed rights to the material. For example, "The Releasor waives any right to further compensation or claims arising from the use of the photograph." This term prevents the releasor from seeking further benefits or making legal claims after the release has been granted, thereby allowing the releasee to use the material without fear of future legal challenges.

Endorsement Disclaimer

The endorsement disclaimer clause ensures that the use of a photograph does not imply any endorsement, sponsorship, or affiliation by the property owner (releasor). It clarifies that the photograph can be used under the agreed terms but must not be portrayed in a way that suggests the property owner's approval or support of the photographer's (releasee's) products, services, or messages. A clause of this kind might provide as follows: "This photograph is used for illustrative purposes only and does not imply any endorsement, sponsorship, or affiliation by the property owner of the messages associated with this photograph."[1]

Representations and Warranties

The representations and warranties clause in a release agreement includes declarations by the releasor about their rights concerning the image. This term assures the releasee that the releasor has the authority to grant the release and that the image does not infringe on any third-party rights. For example, "The Releasor represents and warrants that they are the sole owner of the photograph and have the full authority to grant this release." This clause provides legal assurance that the releasee is obtaining the rights from a legitimate source, protecting them from potential legal disputes.

In the usual course, the releasee also provides representations or warranties as part of a release agreement. These declarations typically assure the releasor that the releasee will use the image according to the agreed terms and within the specified scope. For instance, the releasee might represent and warrant that they will not use the image in a defamatory, libelous, or otherwise unlawful manner. This mutual assurance helps protect both parties' interests and ensures the image is used responsibly and legally.

1 The purpose of this clause is to prevent any false or misleading impressions that the property owner supports, approves, or is affiliated with the product, service, or message being promoted using the photograph.

Indemnification

The indemnification clause in a release agreement is a commitment by the releasor to compensate the releasee for any losses or damages arising from the use of the released material. This term protects the releasee from legal claims related to the photograph, ensuring that any issues originating from the releasor's ownership, or actions do not affect the releasee. For example, "The Releasor agrees to indemnify and hold harmless the Releasee from any claims arising from the use of the photograph." This clause provides a safeguard for the releasee against potential legal liabilities.

In a typical release agreement, it is not uncommon for the releasee to also provide commitments to the releasor regarding indemnification. This means the releasee may agree to compensate the releasor for any losses, damages, or legal claims that might arise from the releasee's use of the image beyond the agreed terms. For example, the releasee might agree to indemnify the releasor if the image is used in a defamatory or unlawful manner. By agreeing to mutual indemnification, both parties are safeguarded and can trust that the material will be handled properly and within the agreed terms.

Termination Clause

The termination clause in a release agreement specifies the conditions under which the agreement can be ended by either party. For instance, it might state:

> Either party may terminate this agreement with written notice if there is mutual consent, a material breach not corrected within 30 days, failure to make required payments within 15 days of the due date, misuse of the photograph contrary to agreed terms, or if new legal regulations require termination. Upon termination, the Releasee must immediately stop using the photograph, and either return or destroy all copies. Any rights or obligations accrued prior to termination will continue to be enforceable after termination.

Governing Law

The governing law clause in a release agreement specifies which jurisdiction's laws will apply to interpret and enforce the terms of the release. For example, "This release shall be governed by and construed in accordance with the laws of the Province of Ontario." This clause ensures that any legal disputes or interpretations of the agreement will be resolved using the specified jurisdiction's legal framework, providing clarity and predictability for both parties.

Signature and Date

The signature and date term formalizes the agreement and indicates mutual consent to the terms. This term requires the signatures of both the releasor and the releasee, along with the date of signing. For example, "Signed this 5th day of July 2022. [Releasor's Signature], [Releasee's Signature]." Signatures and dates confirm that both parties agree to the terms and that the release is legally binding.

By including these detailed terms, a release agreement becomes a comprehensive and legally binding document that clearly defines the rights and responsibilities of both parties and helps avoid future disputes.

When a Building Is Incidental in the Image

A property owner has the right to control how their property is depicted and used commercially. A release ensures you have permission to use the image in a way that respects these rights. What if the building is only an incidental part of the larger image?

When an identifiable building is only an incidental part of a larger image, a release might not be necessary. To determine if a release is needed, consider these questions:

1. What is the main subject of the photograph? Is the building the focus, or just part of the background?
2. Does the building dominate the photograph or is it a minor element?
3. Was the photograph taken to showcase the building, or to capture another subject like people or events?
4. Is the building easily recognizable and could it imply endorsement if used commercially?

These considerations help decide if a property release is required.[2] If the building is not the focal point, occupies only

2 The more recognizable the building, the higher the likelihood that viewers may perceive that the building owner is endorsing the product when it is used in a commercial context.

a minor part of the composition, and the primary intent was to capture another subject, it is likely incidental. However, if there is any doubt it is advisable to obtain a release, especially if the image will be used for commercial purposes.

Summary

A release is generally required based on how the photograph will be used, whether it features a building or an identifiable person. The key consideration is whether the photograph is intended for personal, editorial, or commercial use. For personal or editorial purposes, a release may not be necessary. However, for commercial use, such as in advertisements or promotions, you need to obtain a release from both property owners and any identifiable individuals in the photograph. This ensures legal protection and respects privacy rights. This provides security for all parties and ensures the proper use of the image.

10

Remedies for Copyright Infringement

Overview

Copyright infringement occurs when someone uses, copies, distributes, or displays a copyrighted work without the permission of the copyright holder. For example, suppose a professional photographer takes a series of high-quality photographs of a popular tourist destination. These photographs are uploaded to their website, where they are sold as prints and digital downloads. Without the photographer's permission, a travel agency downloads these images and uses them in their marketing campaigns across social media, in print brochures, and on their official website to promote vacation packages. Despite being contacted by the photographer the travel agency continues to use the images without obtaining a proper licence or paying for them. As the copyright owner you have the right to decide how your photograph will be used. If someone uses your images without your permission, that is copyright infringement.

Relief That Can Be Granted

The *Copyright Act*[1] allows for different types of relief. Section 34(1) provides as follows:

> **34 (1)** Where copyright has been infringed, the owner of the copyright is, subject to this Act, entitled to all remedies by way of injunction, damages, accounts, delivery up and otherwise that are or may be conferred by law for the infringement of a right.

The Act provides various remedies if the copyright has been infringed. The copyright owner can: (1) send a letter demanding that the person stop infringing the copyright; and (2) bring a court proceeding asking for (a) an injunction (b) damages, and (c) an accounting of profits.

Cease and Desist Letter

Sometimes the copyright problem can be solved simply by sending a letter informing the person that you hold the copyright in the photograph, and they are infringing your rights. The person may not be aware they are infringing your rights and will agree to your request rather than face

---

1 RSC 1985, c C-42.

the possibility of litigation. If the person does not respond or refuses to comply with your request, you may need to bring a court proceeding to enforce your request.

Injunctions

Although you are not required to register your copyright, registering it can assist if you need to bring the matter to court. Copyright registration provides evidence that you own the copyright, and provides a rebuttable presumption that copyright exists in the work.

In certain circumstances it may be desirable to seek an interim injunction. An interim injunction is a court order that restrains a party from continuing certain actions until a final decision is made by the court. This can minimize further damages or losses while the legal proceeding is ongoing. In other words, an interim injunction, if granted, would require the travel agency to stop using your image until the court can determine if you are entitled to a permanent injunction.

Disgorgement of Profits

The goal of an "accounting of profits" is to ensure that the infringer does not financially benefit from the unauthorized use of the copyrighted material. An accounting acts as a deterrent against future infringements and compensates the copyright holder for the wrongful use of their work.

In this case the court can order the travel agency to provide detailed financial records showing the revenue and profits directly attributable to the use of the images. This involves identifying all income streams and benefits that resulted from the unauthorized use of the copyrighted photographs.

The travel agency is allowed to deduct legitimate business expenses directly related to the generation of the profits from the infringing activity. However, only reasonable and necessary expenses are considered, and the travel agency bears the burden of proving these expenses.

Once the profits attributable to the infringement are calculated and any allowable expenses are deducted, the travel agency must pay the net profits to the photographer.

Seizure and Destruction of Infringing Copies

Section 34(1) of the *Copyright Act* grants copyright owners the right to seek the surrender of the unauthorized copies of the photographs. The court may order the travel agency to deliver up all infringing copies of the photographs and any materials used to create them. These materials can be destroyed to prevent further infringement.

Damages

If you have suffered a financial loss because of the infringement, you can ask the court for a damages award.

In cases of this kind, you are asking the court to put you in the same position you would have been in if the infringement had not occurred. There are two different approaches to damages: (1) general damages and (2) statutory damages.

Damages and Profits

The photographer can seek compensation for actual damages suffered due to the infringement, including lost sales and licensing fees. In addition to establishing your losses, section 35 of the *Copyright Act* permits the court to award part of the infringer's profits in certain circumstances.

Putting together the evidence necessary to establish the actual loss suffered can be a complicated and expensive process. It may require the retention of one or more experts to review the nature of your business, how the infringement caused the loss, and calculate what your damages are. Establishing the extent of profits that is attributable to the infringement would also require expert evidence.

Statutory Damages

Under the *Copyright Act* the photographer also has the option of electing to ask for "statutory damages." Under the damage's provisions, you are not required to prove the damages in the same way as with general damages. You must prove that your copyright was infringed, and if it was, the Act sets out a range of damages that can be awarded for commercial and non-commercial infringements. The damages range between $500 and $20,000 for each work infringed where the infringement was done for commercial purposes.[2] Where the infringement was for non-commercial purposes, the damages range between $100 and $5,000 for all works infringed.[3] The court looks at a variety of factors when exercising its discretion within the range, such as the good faith or bad faith of the infringer, and the conduct of the parties throughout the proceeding.[4]

Moral Rights

In addition to statutory damages, the court can award damages for infringement of the plaintiff's moral rights. In *Collett v Northland Art Company*[5] the court found that the defendant produced inferior versions of the plaintiff's image, in significant quantities, attributing the artwork to another artist, and then sold the inferior artwork into the same marketplace in which the plaintiff carried on business. Ten thousand dollars was awarded for infringement of the plaintiff's moral rights.

---

2 Section 38.1(1)(a).

3 Section 38.1(1)(b).

4 See *Collett v Northland Art Company Canada Inc et al* Federal Court, 6 November 2017, where the court considers s 38.1(5).

5 *Ibid* at paras 67–68.

Exemplary and Punitive Damages

Electing to proceed using the statutory damages route does not affect the right of the copyright holder to claim exemplary or punitive damages.[6] In the *Collett* decision[7] the court also had to consider whether punitive damages should be awarded. The court concluded punitive damages should be awarded, based upon the follow factors:

> The infringing activity in this case was planned and deliberate. It was motivated by profit. It was not limited to a single incident or occurrence. [The Defendant] was well aware of the infringing activity and sought to conceal the activity.[8]

Punitive damages in the amount of $25,000 were awarded.

Costs and Legal Fees

Costs refer to the expenses incurred by a party in the legal proceeding, including expert fees, expenses for gathering and preparing evidence, and court fees. Legal fees cover the services provided by your lawyer.

The court has discretion in awarding costs and legal fees. The decision is often based on factors such as the conduct of

---

6 *Copyright Act*, s 38.1(7).

7 *Collett v Northland Art Company Canada Inc et al* Federal Court, 6 November 2017.

8 *Ibid* at para 73.

the parties during the litigation, the complexity of the case, and the outcome of the case.

In a case like this, the court would review the conduct of both parties during the litigation. If the photographer's lawyer acted reasonably and attempted to settle the dispute out of court, and the publishing company ignored these attempts, the court could order the company to pay damages to the photographer, and a substantial part of their costs and legal fees.

11

Protecting Yourself Against Copyright Infringement

Copyright Infringement

Copyright law protects your photographs from unauthorized use. Copyright infringement occurs if a person uses, copies, or distributes a copyrighted photograph without the permission of the creator or the holder of the copyright. Infringement can be either direct or indirect. Direct infringement occurs when someone does something with the image that only the copyright owner has the right to do. For example, this might include making a copy of, or authorizing the making of a copy of a photograph, without the owner's consent.

Indirect infringement involves selling or distributing a work the person knows or should know will infringe the copyright. In other words, the person may not have made the original copies of the copyrighted photographs, but they are now selling copies of the copies. If you bring a copyright infringement claim, you have the burden of establishing that your copyright was infringed. Once you establish that, the onus switches to the defendant to justify their use of the photograph.

Register the Copyright

Not everyone will honour your rights or play by the rules, and unauthorized use of your photographs is a constant risk. However, there are ways to minimize the misuse of your photographs. As a photographer, you have copyright protection in your image the instant you take the picture. You do not need to place a copyright notice, the international copyright symbol ©, on your photograph to have copyright protection, and formal registration of your photograph is not required. However, displaying the international copyright symbol © gives you additional protection both in Canada and internationally. Copyright "registration" is not expensive and is beneficial for two reasons. Registration serves as notice to the public that you hold copyright in the photograph and can also help establish ownership if you need to bring a legal action seeking a remedy when someone has infringed your copyright. Copyright registrations are done through the Canadian Intellectual Property Office (CIPO) website.[1]

---

1 Canadian Intellectual Property Office (CIPO), Place du Portage I, 50 Victoria Street, Room C-114 Gatineau, QC K1A 0C9, and online: https://ised-isde.canada.ca/site/canadian-intellectual-property-office/en.

International Protection – Berne Convention

The *Copyright Act*[2] is federal legislation and applies across Canada. Outside of Canada, each country has their own copyright law. If someone infringes your copyright in Canada, you assert your rights under the Canadian *Copyright Act*. However, if someone infringes your copyright in United States, for example, United States copyright law applies. Canada's copyright law will not be enforced in United States.

To harmonize copyright protection, nearly 180 countries have ratified the Berne Convention for the Protection of Literary and Artistic Works, which is administered by the World Intellectual Property Organization (WIPO).[3] The Berne Convention is an international treaty that deals with copyright law. Established in 1886 and administered by WIPO, the Convention provides for the protection of works and the rights of their creators across the member countries. The convention has been revised multiple times, with the most recent amendment made in 1979. It remains one of the most important international agreements in copyright law, influencing copyright legislation in member states and promoting the global protection of creative works.

The Convention sets minimum standards for the protection of copyrighted works, including photographs. Because Canada is a signatory to the Convention, Canadian citizens

---

2 RSC 1985, c C-42.

3 World Intellectual Property Organization (WIPO) 34, chemin des Colombettes CH-1211 Geneva 20 Switzerland, and online: https://www.wipo.int.

enjoy copyright protection in all the countries that have signed the Convention. The Convention provides that copyright protection is granted automatically[4] to qualifying works without the need to register your copyright. This means that your images are protected as soon as they are created and fixed in a tangible form. Creators from member countries are granted the same rights and protections in other member countries as the citizens of that member country.[5] In summary, the Berne Convention does not offer direct enforcement of your rights. However, it establishes the principles and rights that enable you as the photographer to enforce your copyright interest in member countries.

Protecting Your Rights

What steps should you take if you discover that several of your photographs are being sold online on a small e-commerce website without your permission? How do you go about enforcing your rights?

First, try to identify the person or business behind the website, and gather evidence to document the unauthorized use of your images. Consider collecting screenshots or infringing listings, communications with the infringer, and any other relevant information.

Start by sending a cease-and-desist letter to the business or individual who is selling your images without your

4 Article 5(2).
5 Article 5(1).

permission. The letter should identify what the alleged infringement is, including details of the copyrighted works involved. State the legal basis for the cease-and-desist demand including any relevant copyright law. Demand compliance and set out the actions that must be taken, providing a reasonable timeframe for compliance. Clearly communicate the potential consequences of non-compliance, including the possibility of legal action to enforce your rights. Include contact information such as your name, address, phone number, and email address to facilitate communication and possible further discussion. You should include any relevant documentary evidence supporting your claim for infringement, including copies of the copyrighted images.

If the infringing activity continues after the cease-and-desist letter, you should consider pursuing legal action against the infringer. Some law firms specialize in intellectual property matters, and you can seek their legal advice for further assistance. Litigation is a very expensive option unless it can be justified because the size of the damages incurred is significant.

Another option is to seek assistance from organizations or agencies that specialize in copyright enforcement, both domestically and internationally. For example, copyright enforcement agencies[6] offer services such as monitoring for infringement, issuing cease-and-desist letters, pursuing legal action against infringers, and facilitating takedown

---

6 For example, see Pixsy, online: https://www.pixsy.com or Copytrack, online: info@copytrack.com.

requests. The photographer pays a monthly subscription fee for the monitoring service, and if the agency identifies an infringement and successfully recovers damages, they take a pre-agreed percentage of the recovered amount as their fee.

Additionally, government bodies can provide valuable information and resources for dealing with copyright infringement. In Canada, the Canadian Intellectual Property Office (CIPO) is available, while in the United States, you can contact the United States Copyright Office. In Ontario the Law Society of Ontario has a lawyer referral service and will provide the name of a lawyer in Ontario who handles the kind of legal issues you are facing.[7] In other provinces you can likely get similar advice about retaining a lawyer knowledgeable in this area.

Avoiding Copyright Infringement

When photographers post images on social media sites, they retain the copyright in their work, which grants them exclusive rights to reproduce, distribute, and display their images. Uploading an image to a social media platform requires you to agree to the platform's terms of service, which includes a licensing agreement. The licensing

7 The Law Society of Ontario lawyer referral service can be contacted toll free at 1-855-947-5255; see online: http://www.findlegalhelp.ca. Pro Bono Ontario offers a free legal advice hotline for up to thirty minutes of legal advice and assistance. The toll-free number is 1-855-255-7256; see online: https://www.probonoontario.org/hotline/.

agreement grants the site the right to use your images in various ways, as outlined in their terms of service.

The photographer still retains the right to license it to others. However, you are granting the platform very broad licensing rights. For example, the agreement you make with Facebook[8] grants the platform sweeping rights to use your image. When you post content on Facebook, you grant Facebook a non-exclusive, transferable, sub-licensable, royalty-free, worldwide licence to use your content. This licence allows Facebook to use your content in connection with their services, which includes displaying, distributing, and potentially modifying the content. Facebook can also sub-license your content to third parties, such as advertisers, who may use it in their promotional materials. In other words, this allows Facebook to license your photographs without your approval to a third party anywhere in the world for free.

Similarly, Instagram's terms[9] of use provide that:

> When you share, post, or upload content that is covered by intellectual property rights (like photographs or videos) on or in connection with our Service, you hereby grant to us a non-exclusive, royalty-free, transferable, sub-licensable, worldwide license to host, use, distribute, modify, run, copy, publicly perform or display, translate, and create derivative works of your content (consistent with your privacy and application settings).

---

8 See Facebook's terms of service online: https://www.facebook.com/terms.php.

9 See Instagram's terms of service online: https://help.instagram.com/581066165581870.

Again, Instagram's right to use your photographs is very broadly worded. There is nothing that prevents Instagram from sub-licensing your pictures to an advertiser and getting paid for the use of your photographs when you are not getting paid.

In summary, when you post your images on social media sites, you grant the platforms very broad rights, including the right to sub-license your content in multiple ways. The widespread distribution of your photographs facilitated by these platforms makes it easier for others to download and misuse your images without your consent.

Making Copyright Infringement More Difficult

There are several ways you can discourage someone from using your photographs without your consent.

Watermark Your Photographs

One way is to watermark your photographs. What is a watermarking? A watermark is an image, logo, or signature of some kind that is superimposed on a photograph.

The watermark can make it easier to identify your work and promotes your brand. However, watermarking does not always protect against copyright infringement. There are ways to take the watermark out of the photograph using cropping or certain kinds of software. Another problem is that the watermark becomes a distraction and can take away from the impact of the image, and it may discourage someone from using your photograph.

Use Low-Resolution Images

Another way to discourage people from using your images illegally is to upload only low-resolution versions to social media sites. Low-resolution images are less appealing for unauthorized copying due to their reduced quality. Potential infringers may be less inclined to use poor-quality images because when enlarged, these images have a blurry or pixelated appearance. By keeping high-quality original versions protected, you minimize the risk of unauthorized copying.

Edit EXIF Data

Exchangeable Image File (EXIF) data is generated automatically when you take a photograph with a DSLR (Digital Single-Lens Reflex) or digital camera. This data includes information such as shutter speed, image dimensions, and the camera model used. You can also add your name and a copyright notice to this data, making it easier to prove your ownership if the photograph is stolen. However, it is important to note that a sophisticated thief may know how to remove EXIF data from the image.

Digital Locks

The *Copyright Act* provides for digital locks, which are known as technological protection measures (TPMs).[10] A digital lock is a special code or key that keeps your photographs

10 See ss 41, 41.1, 41.11, 41.12, 41.121, 41.13, 41.14, and 41.15 of the *Copyright Act*

safe from being copied or used without your permission. This code acts like a lock that only allows access when the right key is used. Usually, the key is a password of some kind. In this way you can make sure that only people you allow, can access or view your images. However, there are certain limited exceptions that allow for the circumvention of a TPM.[11]

Image Protection Services

There are services available that can help monitor the internet for copyright infringement of your images. For example, Pixsy uses advanced technology to continuously scan websites, social media platforms, and online marketplaces for unauthorized use of your photographs. When Pixsy detects a potential infringement, it notifies the photographer and provides details about the unauthorized use, including the location and the platform where the image appears. Pixsy will also assist in enforcing your copyright by sending cease-and-desist letters, issuing takedown notices, and, if necessary, pursuing legal action. In addition, they will try to negotiate a settlement with the infringer and seek legal remedies through litigation if negotiations fail.

11 For example, under s 41.16(1) of the *Copyright Act* circumventing a technological protection device is allowed where a person has a perceptual disability if certain criteria are met.

12

Legal Considerations for Different Types of Photography

Overview

There are different legal considerations you should be aware of, depending on the type of photography in which you are engaging. For instance, street photography requires careful attention to privacy and consent issues. In contrast, landscape photography, which focuses on nature and scenery, raises issues such as requiring permission from private landowners to access their property. Understanding these legal issues is crucial if you want to avoid legal disputes. We will review several types of photography and highlight the legal issues associated with each.

Portrait Photography

Portrait photography centres on capturing the likeness, personality, and character of individuals, families, or groups. This genre encompasses both formal studio portraits and candid snapshots and can be captured in various settings such as indoor studios, outdoor locations, or everyday environments. Photographers utilize techniques like lighting, composition, posing, and interaction with subjects to create artistic and memorable images that convey the essence of the people being photographed. There are specific legal issues to be aware of in portrait photography.

A model release is required to ensure that both the photographer and the subject understand their rights and responsibilities regarding the use of the images. The release should indicate that the subject consents to the use of their likeness in the photograph taken by the photographer. The release should address the scope of the use. Are there any limitations on where and how the photographs can be used? For example, are the photographs only for personal use, or is the photographer permitted to use the images in their promotional materials? If the photographs will only be used for a certain project or within a specific timeframe, this should be set out in the release as well. The release should include a provision releasing the photographer from liability for any claims arising from the use of the photographs.

In Canada, individuals have a reasonable expectation of privacy in private settings such as homes and other private places. If you are photographing someone in a private setting, you should obtain their consent for the photography session. The model release should explicitly state that the subject consents to the photographer entering the home for the agreed-upon photography session to take pictures. This makes sure the photographer's actions and presence in the private setting are legally compliant.

Photographing minors involves additional legal considerations required to protect the interests and rights of children. Consent must be obtained from a parent or legal guardian, and this consent should be documented in a model release. Laws and regulations, such as child protection legislation, sometimes impose guidelines on the use and distribution of images of minors.[1] Photographers must handle images of minors with care, ensuring they are used appropriately.

Usage rights describe how a client or third party is allowed to use the photographs. These rights should be clearly explained in the contract, specifying where and how the photographs can be used, such as in advertisements or on social media, how long they can be used, and any location restrictions.[2] Having usage rights clearly set out in the release help avoid unauthorized use, and ensures the photographer and client agree on the terms. For instance, a photographer may allow a client to use a photograph for a specific charity campaign but not for resale or licensing to others. Proper documentation of these rights protects the photographer's work and income.

1 For example, see s 122 of Ontario's *Child, Youth and Family Services Act*, SO 2017, c 14, Sch 1 (CYFSA).

2 Location restrictions may limit the use of the image to certain geographic areas, venues, or types of media.

Location restrictions refer to specific limitations on where photographs can be used or displayed based on the agreement between the photographer and the client. These restrictions may limit the use of the image to certain geographic areas, venues, or types of media. For example, a photograph might only be used in local advertising, or for a specific event, but not across multiple platforms. These restrictions are important to avoid unauthorized use and protect the photographer's rights.

When taking photographs on private property or places with specific rules, photographers need to get permission. This might mean getting a location release from the property owner or applying for a permit to photograph in places like a city park. If you do not get permission, you could face legal problems, such as being accused of trespassing. Location permissions make sure you are allowed to be there and use the photographs you take. Some places also have certain rules, such as not allowing photography in certain areas, or requiring you to credit the location when sharing the images.

Sports Photography

Sports photography focuses on capturing athletes in action during sporting events. It not only records their physical movements but also highlights the exciting and emotional moments, showing teamwork, intensity, joy, and disappointment. This type of photography aims to freeze dynamic scenes that convey the energy and emotions of the sport.

Several legal issues can arise. With this type of photography, you may be taking pictures of recognizable athletes, coaches, and spectators. While individuals in a public setting usually have a lower expectation of privacy, if you are planning on using the photograph of an identifiable individual for commercial purposes, you need to obtain a model release that addresses such things as the right to use the player's likeness, where the image will be used, and the compensation to be paid.

Photographs taken at sports events may also capture trademarks, team logos, or other symbols. You need to be cautious about how you use images of this kind. For instance, the law allows for the incidental inclusion of a trademark in an image. However, it is important to note the specific circumstances must be considered in each case to determine whether the trademark is only incidental. If the trademark in the image is more than just incidental, you should be getting a release.

If you are taking photographs in a major sports venue, there will likely be rules that address how photographs taken at the venue can be used. In some cases, you may find that you are not permitted to sell the photograph for commercial purposes at all. The Rogers Centre in Toronto even has guidelines about the size of lenses you can use when you are at a game. Cameras with detachable lenses longer that three inches are prohibited.[3]

You also need to keep in mind the property rights associated with the venue where you want to take the photographs. Property rights allow the owner of sports centres to control different aspects of the activities in the building.

---

3 *Rogers Centre Information Guide 2024.*

For example, the owner can control who has access to the building or impose restrictions on what activities can take place in the building. These rules may specify areas where photography is permitted, or not allowed, or set limits on how the photograph can be used.

If you are planning on taking a photograph in a sports centre, you should be conducting research in advance to understand what you can or cannot do with the photographs you take.

Wildlife Photography

This type of photography targets wildlife in their natural habitat. Wildlife photographers try to document special moments and behaviours. This might include a predator hunting its prey, a mother caring for her young, or animals interacting with their environment.

You should familiarize yourself with federal, provincial, and local regulations governing wildlife photography in the location where you are planning on taking your photographs. There may be laws and regulations to protect wildlife and minimize disturbances to animals in their natural habitat. For example, in Banff National Park you must stay a certain distance away from wildlife: thirty metres for deer, elk, sheep, and moose, and one hundred metres for bears, wolves, cougars, and coyotes.[4] Fines for violating wildlife

4 See Banff wildlife guidelines: Government of Canada, "Safely View Wildlife," last modified 23 May 2024, online: https://parks.canada.ca/pn-np/ab/banff/visit/faune-wildlife/espace-space.

protection regulations can vary depending on the severity of the offence. In Banff National Park fines can range from several hundred to several thousand dollars for approaching wildlife too closely. It is essential to familiarize yourself with the wildlife protection regulations before you go on your photo shoot.

Travel Photography

Travel photography focuses on capturing images of the people, cultures, customs, and architecture in other countries. Viewers can experience vicariously the diversity and richness of the planet we inhabit.

When travelling abroad, it's important to be aware of local cultural norms in any foreign country you visit. In some countries, photographing certain subjects or activities may be seen as offensive or disrespectful. In Canada, taking photographs of people in public spaces is generally allowed, but privacy laws differ in other countries. In some places, taking a stranger's photograph without consent might violate their privacy rights. You should also follow copyright and intellectual property laws in the country where you are photographing. This means understanding who owns the rights to the things you photograph, such as artwork, buildings, or other copyrighted content. This includes ensuring you do not use those images in ways that violate local laws, like selling or reproducing them without permission. If you are on private property or in a place of worship, always get permission. For commercial photography, you may need permits or licences. Be cautious when photographing sensitive locations like military bases or government buildings, as this could be mistaken for espionage.

It is very important for you to do your research on issues of this kind before you arrive in the country. Violating local rules may result in fines or other penalties. If you are uncertain about the rules, you can also check with the local authorities.

Landscape Photography

Landscape photographers try to capture the beauty, grandeur, and serenity of the natural world around us. Landscape photography raises several legal issues about which you need to be conscious. Depending on the location you are in, and the type of photography planned, you may need a permit or permission to take your photographs.

For example, if you wish to take photographs on private property you need to obtain permissions from the landowner or property manager. You should ensure that you are familiar with and follow any requirements imposed by the landowner.[5]

5 For a discussion of various issues see above, Chapter 2, Shooting Locations – Private Property.

If you want to take photographs on Indigenous lands[6] or reserves[7] it is important to respect the rights and protocols of the Indigenous community or the authority responsible for those lands, and to obtain necessary permits or permissions for your photography activities. At all times ensure you are respectful of the First Nations' culture, traditions, and land rights.

In national parks and other protected areas certain activities like photography may require permits or permission of some kind. If you plan to take photographs, especially for commercial purposes, you need to investigate what permits are required ahead of time. For example, to minimize the impact on sensitive habitats and wildlife, there may be conditions attached to where you can take the photographs, or when this can be done during the day. Following the rules is necessary to help ensure the landscape, wildlife, and cultural sites are preserved for future generations.

Details about the application process and fee schedule for commercial photography permits can be found in guidelines provided by Parks Canada. These details often include application fees, daily shooting fees, and other conditions for obtaining a permit. For specific information about fees and the application process, you can refer to the

---

6 This term encompasses a broad range of lands and territories traditionally used, occupied, or claimed by Indigenous Peoples in Canada.

7 A reserve, known as an Indian reserve or a First Nations reserve, refers to a tract of land set aside for use and occupancy of a specific Indigenous community or band under the Canadian *Indian Act*, RSC 1985, c I-5.

Parks Canada website or directly contact the park where you intend to conduct your photography.[8]

Street Photography

Street photography is a genre of photography that captures candid moments and scenes in public places. It often focuses on the everyday activities of people, the urban environment, and the interactions between individuals and their surroundings. Sometimes images of public celebrations, cultural events, and parades are the focus. Street photography can also serve to highlight social issues such as homelessness, poverty, and inequality to help raise public awareness and promote change.

When practising street photography, several legal considerations must be considered to ensure compliance with privacy, property, and copyright laws. Photographers have the right to take pictures in public spaces where people generally do not have a reasonable expectation of privacy. However, you must still be mindful of potentially infringing on someone's privacy rights in these settings because privacy concerns can still arise.[9]

Entering private property without permission to take photographs can lead to trespass claims. Photographers must always seek consent before capturing images on

8 See Park's Canada online: https://parks.canada.ca.

9 See *Aubry v Éditions Vice-Versa Inc* [1998] 1 SCR 591.

private property to avoid legal issues related to trespass and invasion of privacy. Obtaining consent protects the photographer and respects the rights of the property owners and occupants, ensuring that all parties are aware of and agree to the intended use of the photographs.

If photographs taken in public spaces are intended for commercial purposes, photographers must obtain a model release from all identifiable individuals in the images. This release grants permission to use their likeness for commercial purposes and will avoid legal disputes over unauthorized use. The need for consent, for example, would arise where images are used in advertisements, promotions, or other commercial contexts.

Photographers must also avoid portraying individuals in a false or misleading light, which could result in a defamation claim. A defamation action can be brought when the published image falsely portrayed the person and caused harm to their reputation, leading to damages for loss of income, emotional distress, or social standing. A photographer should always ensure the depiction of a person is fair and does not present the individual in a false or misleading light that could harm their reputation.

When photographing graffiti or other artwork, photographers must be mindful of copyright laws. The original artist holds the copyright to their work, and using these images for commercial purposes without permission can lead to a copyright infringement claim. It is essential to obtain a release from the artist, if possible, before using such images commercially to ensure compliance with copyright laws.

Food Photography

Food photography usually involves capturing appetizing images of food and beverages for commercial purposes such as marketing and advertising. Food photographers use different techniques such as lighting and composition to create images that showcase the food's appeal.

There are a few important legal issues to consider. First, if the food packaging in your photographs includes trademarks, logos, or designs, using those images without permission could violate the intellectual property rights of the trademark owner. Make sure you have the right to use them. Second, if there are any recognizable people in the photographs, such as chefs, servers, or diners, you will need a model release to legally use their image for commercial purposes. Finally, when using food photographs in marketing, you must avoid false advertising or misrepresentation and comply with advertising standards like those set by Advertising Standards Canada (ASC).

By addressing these legal issues, food photographers can steer clear of potential legal disputes.

Drone Photography

Drone photography involves the use of cameras mounted on unmanned aerial vehicles (UAVs) and offers a fresh and innovative perspective for capturing images. Soaring above the ground, drones unlock views that were once difficult or impossible to achieve, revealing the vastness of

Canada's landscapes, cities, and natural features. Using drones, photographers can capture unique angles, patterns, and compositions, creating stunning and inspiring images.

Drones are regulated by the federal government under the *Aeronautics Act*[10] ensuring uniformity in all provinces and territories across Canada. While the regulation of drones is a federal responsibility, provinces and municipalities may enact complementary rules related to such things as privacy and trespassing provided it does not conflict with the federal legislation.

There are several legal considerations that come into play when operating a drone to be aware of.

Be careful not to invade someone's privacy. For example, imagine a homeowner relaxing in their fenced backyard, hidden from neighbours and passersby. If a drone flies over, records the person sunbathing without their consent, and the footage is shared on social media, it violates their privacy. The homeowner had a reasonable expectation of privacy in their backyard, and the drone operator's actions crossed that line.

If you fly your drone in airspace over private property without consent, you could face an action for trespass. Under the common law, the rights of property owners extend not only to the surface of their land, but also to the airspace above it. These rights are limited to the airspace that is reasonably necessary for the owner's use and

10 RSC 1985, c A-2. See Canadian Aviation Regulations (SOR/96-433) Part IX – Remotely Piloted Aircraft Systems.

enjoyment of their property.[11] Courts have recognized that property owners do not control all the airspace above their land. For example, commercial aviation at high altitudes is not considered a trespass.

When a drone enters this "reasonably necessary" airspace without the property owner's consent, it can constitute a trespass. To avoid potential trespass claims, drone operators should obtain consent before flying over private property and avoid taking images of the property without explicit permission.

Drone operators can also be the subject of a "nuisance" claim. The law of "nuisance" applies to situations where one party's actions unreasonably interfere with another's use or enjoyment of their property. To succeed in a nuisance claim, the interference must cause more than minor inconvenience or discomfort. Drones can create disturbances in a variety of ways. The sound of drone propellers can disturb homeowners, particularly in quiet neighbourhoods or during nighttime operations. Hovering a drone over a backyard or near windows can also be intrusive and upsetting for residents.

Flying a drone carelessly can lead to a negligence claim. For example, imagine a drone operator flying their drone in a public park near a crowded outdoor concert. Instead of following the rule to stay at least thirty metres away from people, they fly the drone over the audience to get aerial footage.[12] The operator loses control, and the drone crashes, hitting someone in the crowd, causing a concussion.

---

11 See *Didow v Alberta Power Ltd* 1988 ABCA 257 at para 37.

12 Drone pilots must follow the rules in the Canadian Aviation Regulations (SOR/96-433). See Part IX – Remotely Piloted Aircraft Systems.

To avoid legal problems, always get permission before flying a drone near private areas and avoid taking photographs where people expect privacy. Be mindful of how your actions might affect others, always respecting their privacy and comfort.

Understanding the legal risks helps drone operators avoid future problems. It is important to stay up to date on laws that apply to drones because they can change. Photographers should regularly check Transport Canada and local aviation websites for the latest rules and updates; take training courses to learn about new legal, technical, and ethical guidelines; and join drone photography groups to share tips and receive advice from other photographers.[13]

13 For additional resources and support, consider consulting organizations like Model Aeronautics Association of Canada (MAAC) or regional drone operator associations. The MAAC is the national governing body for model aviation in Canada. It provides guidance, support, and resources for individuals and organizations involved in flying radio-controlled aircraft, including drones, model airplanes, and other small aerial vehicles.

13

Litigation Risks for Photographers

Overview

Photographers need to be aware of the types of legal claims that can be brought against them, and the steps they can take to protect their work.

Understanding the basics of different legal claims helps you avoid costly, time-consuming problems and ensures that you can identify potential risks early, helping you avoid disputes before they escalate into expensive legal battles. To help you navigate these risks, we will look at common types of lawsuits that can have an impact on photographers and how to avoid them.

Negligence

Negligence claims can be brought against a photographer on a variety of grounds. Negligence refers to the failure to take reasonable care or precautions that a prudent photographer would take in similar circumstances, that results in harm or injury to another person or their property.

If a photographer fails to take proper precautions to ensure the safety of clients during a shoot and someone gets hurt, they could be sued for negligence. For example, if equipment is not secured properly and causes an injury, this might be considered negligence. A photographer can also be held liable if they damage a client's or third party's property during the shoot. Additionally, failing to provide the agreed services, like not showing up for an event or delivering poor-quality images, could lead to a negligence claim for damages.

To establish negligence the plaintiff (the person who has been harmed) must show that: (1) The defendant (the person who caused the harm) owes the plaintiff a duty of care. This means that the defendant had a legal obligation to take reasonable care to avoid causing harm to the plaintiff or their property. (2) The plaintiff must establish that the defendant breached that duty of care by failing to act as a reasonable prudent photographer would in similar circumstances. (3) The plaintiff must prove that the defendant's actions were a direct cause of the plaintiff's injuries or losses. (4) The plaintiff must establish that the defendant's actions were the proximate cause of the plaintiff's injury or loss. This means that the plaintiff must establish that the harm the plaintiff suffered was a reasonably foreseeable consequence of the defendant's breach of duty. (5) The plaintiff must prove that they suffered actual harm because of the defendant's breach of duty. This could include physical injury or financial losses.

To avoid facing claims related to safety, property damage, or failing to deliver services, photographers should take the following steps:

1. Ensure all equipment is properly secured, maintained, and used according to safety standards. Identify any potential hazards at the location and communicate these to clients to prevent accidents.
2. Regularly inspect and maintain cameras, lighting, and other equipment to ensure everything functions correctly and safely.
3. Arrive on time for scheduled shoots and deliver images or services as agreed in the contract.

Following these steps will minimize the risk of potential negligence claims.

Breaching Licensing Agreement Terms

In the context of photography, the licensor is the photographer who owns the copyright and grants permission to use their photographs, while the licensee is the individual or business that receives permission, via a licence, to use the photographs, under agreed-upon terms.

If a licensee does not follow the terms of a licensing agreement, they are in breach of the contract. This could happen if they use the licensed photographs without permission, fail to make required payments, or use the images in ways that go beyond what the agreement allows.

To succeed with a claim for breach of the agreement, the plaintiff must prove several things: (1) They must show that a valid licensing agreement existed between the parties. While these agreements can be oral or written, it is best if they are in writing. (2) The plaintiff must demonstrate that the defendant violated the terms of that agreement. (3) The plaintiff must prove they suffered some type of harm, such as financial losses, harm to their reputation, or missed business opportunities, due to the breach. (4) There must be a direct connection between the defendant's breach and the plaintiff's damages. (5) The plaintiff has a duty to reduce their losses by taking reasonable steps after the breach to minimize any further damage.

How might a dispute based on breach of a licensing agreement arise? Suppose a professional photographer specializing in wildlife photography licenses one of their best-selling photographs of a polar bear to a publishing company to be used in a coffee table book about endangered species. The licensing agreement provides that the photograph can only be used in the specified book and does not allow for any other uses without the photographer's permission. Contrary to the terms of the licensing agreement the publisher allows the photograph to be used in an advertising campaign for luxury excursions to the Arctic. The photograph is prominently displayed on billboards, in social media, and print advertisements.

The photographer can bring a claim based on the written licensing agreement as evidence of the agreed upon terms. The photographer must establish that the publishing company breached the licensing agreement by allowing the photograph to be used for a purpose other than what was specified, the coffee table book. The photographer must establish that they suffered damages or losses due to the unauthorized use of their photograph, and there is a direct causal link between the breach of the licensing agreement and the financial losses or reputational harm they may have suffered. Finally, the photographer would need to establish they took reasonable steps to mitigate the damages by contacting the publishing company as soon as they became aware of what the company was doing.

To minimize the chances of a licensing agreement breach, the licensor should take certain steps:

1. Keep thorough records of every interaction related to the licensing agreement. This includes initial discussions, signed contracts, and any changes (amendments or addendums) made to the original terms.
2. Periodically check how the licensee is using the licensed photographs. This could involve reviewing the licensee's advertising materials, websites, or other platforms where the photographs are displayed.
3. If the photographer discovers that the licensee is using the photographs beyond the scope of the agreement, they should address the issue promptly.

By following these steps, photographers can protect their work, maintain control over how their images are used, and reduce the chances of legal disputes related to licensing agreement violations.

Copyright Infringement

Copyright infringement occurs when someone uses, reproduces, or distributes a photographer's images, without the photographer's permission, in violation their exclusive rights under copyright law.

Suppose a photographer takes a stunning photograph of a sunrise over the mountains early on a winter day and posts it on their website. The owner of a travel agency sees the photograph and decides to use it in an online advertisement without the photographer's consent. The unauthorized use of the photograph constitutes copyright infringement because the photograph is being used without permission or a licence from the photographer. What does the photographer need to bring a copyright infringement claim?

With copyright infringement the plaintiff must establish four elements: (1) The plaintiff must prove that they hold a valid copyright in the image that was copied. The photographer can establish this through their registration of the copyright with the Canadian Intellectual Property Office (CIPO), or other documentary evidence to prove they took the photograph. (2) The plaintiff must demonstrate that the defendant's photograph is substantially like their copyrighted image. This involves comparing the two images in terms of expression, and not just the subject matter. Expression includes aspects such as composition, framing, angle, lighting, colour, subject matter, mood, style, and any other distinctive features. (3) The plaintiff must provide evidence that the alleged infringer copied the copyrighted work. This can be proven through direct evidence such as an admission of copying, or circumstantial evidence, such as access to the copyrighted work and the substantial similarity of the two images. (4) The plaintiff must show that the alleged infringement violates one or more of the exclusive rights granted to copyright holders, such as the right to reproduce the work, produce derivative works, distribute copies, and display the image publicly.

In Canada, to reduce the chances of someone infringing your copyright in a photograph, you can take the following steps:

1. Register your copyright with the Canadian Intellectual Property Office (CIPO). This creates a record proving your ownership and can help if any infringement issues arise.
2. Display a copyright notice (e.g., "© [Your Name] [Year]") on your images, either on your website, portfolio, or directly on the images. While not legally required, it reinforces the fact that the image is protected under copyright law.
3. Place visible watermarks on your photographs when sharing them online. Watermarks deter unauthorized use and clearly signal your ownership of the image.
4. Regularly monitor the internet for unauthorized uses of your images. You can use reverse image search tools like Google Image Search or specialized services to track where your photographs are being used.

5. Keep detailed records of your work, including the dates when photographs were taken, the original files, and metadata. This evidence can support your claim that you hold a valid copyright.

As a photographer, it is also important to ensure that you are not infringing the copyright of others. Copyright infringement does not arise if the copyrighted element is only incidental to the larger photograph.[1] However, taking a photograph of a stage play, for example, and selling the images commercially without consent would infringe on the copyright holder's exclusive right to distribute images of their play.

There are several steps you can take to minimize the chance of being named as a defendant in a copyright infringement claim:

1. When creating your photographs, be careful not to replicate another photographer's work. Even if you share a similar subject, avoid copying the specific way they have composed, framed, or styled the image.
2. If you plan to use another photographer's work, ensure that you obtain a licence to use their images.

---

1 *Copyright Act*, RSC 1985, c C-42, s 30.7:

> It is not an infringement of copyright to incidentally and not deliberately,
>
> (a) include a work or other subject-matter in another work or other subject-matter; or
>
> (b) do any act in relation to a work or other subject-matter that is incidentally and not deliberately included in another work or other subject-matter.

3. If you must use existing photographs, rely on images in the public domain or those licensed under Creative Commons[2] that allow for commercial or personal use.
4. Be cautious when using images found on the internet. Many photographs are copyrighted, even if no explicit copyright notice is present. Instead, use trusted stock photography platforms that clearly define usage rights.
5. If you are using an image provided by a client or third party, verify that they have the rights to the photograph they provide. Otherwise, you could be unknowingly infringing the copyright.

By following these steps, you can safeguard your own images from unauthorized use and minimize the risk of infringing someone else's copyrighted work.

Defamation

Defamation law balances the protection of a person's reputation with the right to freedom of expression. A statement, including a photograph, is defamatory if it lowers the subject's reputation in the eyes of a reasonable person. For example, suppose a tabloid newspaper uses a photograph of an individual that is taken out of context and portrays the person in a false or negative light.

The plaintiff has the burden of establishing that the tabloid's publication of the photograph and accompanying

2 Creative Commons, 171 Second Street, Suite 300, San Francisco, CA 94105, USA, online: https://creativecommons.org.

article was defamatory and resulted in harm to their reputation. In *Grant v Torstar Corp*,[3] the Supreme Court of Canada held that a plaintiff in a defamation action is required to prove three things to obtain judgment and an award of damages. The plaintiff must prove:

> (1) that the impugned words were defamatory, in the sense that they would tend to lower the plaintiff's reputation in the eyes of a reasonable person; (2) that the words in fact referred to the plaintiff; and (3) that the words were published, meaning that they were communicated to at least one person other than the plaintiff.

In a legal action involving photography, substitute the word "photograph" for "words."

Defamation in Canada is treated as a strict liability tort. "The plaintiff is not required to show that the defendant intended to do harm, or even that the defendant was careless. The tort is thus one of strict liability."[4] Instead, the evidence focuses on whether the defamatory statement was made, and whether it referred to the plaintiff.

To minimize the risk of their images being used in a defamatory way, photographers should take the following steps:

1. When granting usage rights to third parties, include clear clauses in your licensing agreements that prohibit the image from being used in defamatory or misleading context.

---

3 2009 SCC 61 at para 28.
4 *Ibid*.

2. Regularly check how your photographs are being used, especially if licensed to media outlets. If you see your image used in a defamatory manner, address it immediately by contacting the publisher and seeking legal advice.
3. Be selective about where and how your photographs are distributed. If a publication or client has a history of defamatory content, it may be best to avoid working with them to reduce the chance of your images being misused.

To minimize the risk of a defamation claim being brought against you for your photographs, it is essential to follow these key practices:

1. Be mindful of the context in which your photograph is taken and how it may be perceived by others. Ensure that the photograph does not portray individuals in a misleading or false way that could harm their reputation.
2. When photographing people, especially in public, avoid capturing images that could easily be interpreted negatively, such as someone in a compromising or awkward situation, which could harm their reputation.
3. If you are responsible for captions or accompanying text, ensure that it accurately reflects the image without misleading or misrepresenting the person or scene. False or exaggerated captions can turn an otherwise neutral image into a defamatory statement.

By following these rules, photographers can protect themselves from defamation claims and ensure their work is not used to harm someone's reputation.

Appropriation of Personality

As a photographer you should be aware of the tort called appropriation of personality. A person has control over their name and image, and how it can be used for commercial purposes. The appropriation of personality tort allows a person to sue for damages if their image has been used for commercial purposes without their consent.

You are allowed to take photographs of public figures, celebrities, professional athletes, and performers for personal enjoyment. However, those individuals have an exclusive right to market their image if it is being used commercially, for example, selling a product or service.

This tort[5] arises where a photograph is taken of a celebrity and is used without the celebrity's consent in a way that makes it look like they are endorsing a commercial activity of some kind. A person has the right to control the use of their image, and the commercial benefit that flow from the use of their image belong to that person.

To establish a claim for appropriation of personality in Canada, the following elements must be established: (1) The plaintiff must demonstrate that the defendant used a recognizable aspect of their personality, such as their image, name, or likeness. (2) The use of the plaintiff's personality must be for a commercial purpose. The court emphasized that the tort is focused on the unauthorized commercial exploitation of a person's identity. (3) The defendant must

---

5 *Krouse v Chrysler Canada Ltd* (1973) 1 OR (2d) 225 (CA).

have used the plaintiff's likeness without their consent. (4) The plaintiff must show that they suffered damage because of the unauthorized use. This can include financial loss, harm to reputation, or emotional distress.

There are two cases that illustrate what appropriation of personality is and is not. In *Athans v Canadian Adventure Camps Ltd et al*,[6] the plaintiff, Athans, was a professional athlete who was recognized nationally and internationally for his water-skiing skills. One of the defendants, Canadian Adventure Camps, operated a commercial summer camp for children and featured water-skiing as part of its program. For promotional purposes, it published a brochure and an advertisement containing a graphic representation based upon a photograph displaying the celebrity's "trademark" image. This was intentionally incorporated into the camp's advertising materials to promote its water-skiing program.

The court found that the commercial use of the plaintiff's image, without his consent, constituted appropriation of personality and he was entitled to damages equal to what he would have received in the market for permission to use his image.

In *Gould Estate v Stoddart Publishing Co*,[7] the court reached a different conclusion on whether the fact situation supported a claim based on the tort of appropriation of personality. The case involved the estate of Glenn Gould, a world-renowned pianist, suing the publisher of a book that contained photographs of Gould taken forty years earlier at

6 (1977) 17 OR (2d) 425 (HCJ).
7 (1996) 30 OR (3d) 520 (Gen Div).

the start of his career. The estate sought damages, in part, under the appropriation of personality tort.

The court found that the publisher was not liable, distinguishing between using a photograph for commercial purposes and using a photograph to satisfy the public's interest in knowing more about the person photographed. The court noted that the tort "has not been successfully invoked in cases where the activity in question consists of thoughts, ideas, newsworthy events or matters of public interest."[8]

The judge further explained the "sales vs. subject" distinction in determining whether the appropriation of personality tort has been committed. "Sales" involves the commercial exploitation of an image, where the celebrity's identity is used to sell a product. This contrasts with situations where the celebrity is the "subject" of the work, such as in a biography. In these cases, the use of the image does not fall within the scope of the tort.

To reduce the risk of being sued for appropriation of personality, follow these key steps: (1) Always obtain explicit consent from the person whose image you plan to use for commercial purposes. This applies to everyone, including public figures, celebrities, or any recognizable individual in your photographs. (2) Use a detailed release form for commercial use that clearly outlines the terms of how the image will be used. This ensures that both you and the person in the photograph agree regarding its use and prevents potential misunderstandings or legal disputes.

---

8 *Ibid.*

Be alert to the distinction between using a person's image to promote sales, and using the image for editorial purposes, such as in a biography or news story. If your photograph is being used to report on a public figure, rather than to sell a product, this should not create a problem.

Common Law Invasion of Privacy Torts

The invasion of privacy tort embraces various legal principles aimed at protecting the privacy rights of individuals from unjustified intrusion by others. There are two different torts you should be aware of: (1) public disclosure of private facts and (2) intrusion upon seclusion.

Public Disclosure of Private Facts

This type of claim involves the unauthorized disclosure to the public of private information about an individual, causing embarrassment, humiliation, or harm to a person's reputation. In *Jane Doe 72511 v NM*,[9] the plaintiff was involved in a relationship with the defendant. During their relationship, Jane Doe shared intimate images with NM under the expectation of privacy. After their relationship ended, NM shared these images online without Jane Doe's consent, leading to significant emotional distress and harm to Jane Doe.

---

9 2018 ONSC 6607.

Jane Doe filed a lawsuit against NM, alleging that his actions constituted a violation of her privacy rights, specifically under the emerging tort of "public disclosure of private facts." The Ontario Superior Court of Justice recognized this tort and ruled in favour of Jane Doe, awarding her damages for the harm she suffered due to the unauthorized distribution of her private images.

The court held that to meet the test the plaintiff must establish the following: (1) conduct that is flagrant and outrageous; (2) calculated to produce harm; and (3) resulting in a visible and provable injury.[10] A malicious purpose is not required to establish this tort.[11]

Jane Doe is a landmark decision in Canadian law because it was one of the first to formally recognize the tort of public disclosure of private facts, providing a legal remedy for individuals whose private information has been disclosed without their consent.

This case highlights the importance of safeguarding personal privacy, especially in relationships where private information is shared with the expectation of confidentiality. This case serves as a powerful reminder that individuals have the right to control how their private information is shared, and violating this right can result in serious legal repercussions. The lesson to be learned is clear: respecting privacy is not just a moral obligation but is also a legal one.

Photographers should always get explicit written consent before sharing or publishing any private or sensitive

10 *Ibid* at para 26.
11 *Ibid* at para 27.

information about an individual. The consent should address how the photographs will be used and with whom they will be shared.

Intrusion Upon Seclusion

This type of claim is based upon the unauthorized disclosure or dissemination of sensitive or private information about someone. The public disclosure causes embarrassment, humiliation, or harm to a person's reputation. In *Jones v Tsige*[12] the plaintiff and the defendant did not know each other, but they worked for different branches of the same bank and the defendant was in a common law relationship with the plaintiff's ex-husband. For about four years, the defendant used her workplace computer to access the plaintiff's personal bank accounts more than a hundred times, but did not publish, distribute, or record the information in any way. When the plaintiff discovered the conduct, she brought an action for damages for invasion of privacy

The Ontario Court of Appeal found in her favour and set out the test as follows: (1) the defendant's conduct must be intentional or reckless; (2) the defendant must have invaded, without lawful justification, the plaintiff's private affairs or concerns; (3) a reasonable person would regard the invasion as highly offensive causing distress, humiliation, or anguish.[13]

Although the *Jones* case did not involve photography, the same legal principles would apply in the case of a

12 [2012] ONCA 32.
13 *Ibid* at para 71.

photographer. An example of this might be where a clerk installs a hidden camera in a change room of a clothing store, which captured intimate footage of a customer trying on clothes. Once the camera is discovered, the customer could bring an action against the clerk arguing that placing the camera in the change room without their consent constituted an invasion of their privacy.

Photographers should be careful to avoid actions that might be seen as invading someone's privacy. Privacy laws protect individuals from unwanted exposure of their personal lives, and violating these laws can have serious legal consequence. Breaking these laws could result in financial penalties and harm a photographer's reputation. By respecting privacy rights, photographers avoid any legal problems and build trust with their subjects.

Damages Under PIPEDA

The use of an individual's image for commercial purposes without their consent is a breach of the person's privacy rights under the *Personal Information Protection and Electronic Documents Act* (PIPEDA).[14] If you breach the privacy provisions, the legislation provides a mechanism for individuals to seek remedies through the Office of the Privacy Commissioner of Canada, and subsequently in the Federal Court.[15]

14 SC 2000, c 5.

15 Depending on the jurisdiction provincial privacy laws may apply. British Columbia, Alberta, and Quebec each have their own privacy legislation that governs the collection, use, and disclosure of personal information in the private section which should be read together with PIPEDA.

For example, suppose that an advertising agency uses a person's image in a brochure for the sale of a product without the person's consent. The person can file a complaint with the privacy commissioner who has the powers to investigate the complaint, including the right to summon witnesses and compel the production of documents. The commissioner can recommend that the advertising agency stop using the person's image and advise the agency to destroy all unauthorized copies of the image. The commissioner can also recommend that the agency provide privacy training to employees as well as develop and enforce stronger privacy policies to prevent future violations.[16]

If the person is not satisfied with the outcome of the Privacy Commissioner's investigation, they can appeal to the Federal Court for a hearing.[17] The Federal Court can award damages, including compensation for humiliation.

Provincial Privacy Acts

British Columbia, Saskatchewan, Manitoba, and Newfoundland and Labrador have their own privacy legislation governing the collection, use, and disclosure of the personal information.[18]

16 See ss 11, 12.1, and 13 of the *Personal Information Protection and Electronic Documents Act*, SC 2000, c 5.

17 Section 14(1) of the *Personal Information Protection and Electronic Documents Act* SC 2000, c 5.

18 *Privacy Act*, RSBC 1996, c 373; *The Privacy Act*, RSS 1978, c P-24; *The Privacy Act*, CCSM c P125; and *Privacy Act*, RSNL 1990, c P-22.

For example, under the British Columbia *Privacy Act*, it is a tort to wilfully and without a claim of right violate the privacy of another person. For a photographer, this means taking and using photographs of individuals without their consent in a way that invades their privacy. Section 1(1) of the Act states: "It is a tort, actionable without proof of damage, for a person, willfully and without a claim of right, to violate the privacy of another."

The invasion must be wilful or reckless, which means that the defendant acted with a clear intention to invade the privacy of the person, or with a reckless disregard for the likelihood that their actions would invade the person's privacy. The court also examines the context, including the relationships between the parties, the setting in which the invasion occurred, and societal norms and expectations of privacy to determine if the invasion was unreasonable.

In *Hollinsworth v BCTV*,[19] the plaintiff, John Hollinsworth, had undergone a hair replacement surgery, which was filmed with his consent by a television crew from BCTV. The footage was intended for use in a documentary on medical procedures. However, several years later, BCTV reused the footage in a different context without obtaining Hollinsworth's consent, showing it in an advertisement for a news program. Hollinsworth claimed that this unauthorized use of the footage violated his privacy rights and sued for invasion of privacy.

19 [1999] 6 WWR 54 (BCCA).

The British Columbia Court of Appeal considered the words "wilfully and without claim of right" and concluded that:

> [T]he word "wilfully" does not apply broadly to any intentional act that has the effect of violating privacy but more narrowly to an intention to do an act which the person doing the act knew or should have known would violate the privacy of another person.[20]

The court went on to define the words "without a claim of right" to mean: ". . . an honest belief in a state of facts which, if it existed, would be a legal justification or excuse. . . ."[21]

In other words, to bring a successful claim under the British Columbia *Privacy Act*, the plaintiff must demonstrate: (1) the defendant's actions were intentional and specifically aimed at violating the person's privacy; and (2) the defendant did not have an honest belief in a set of facts that would justify or excuse their actions.

Summary

It's important for photographers to understand both the legal claims they can bring and those that could be brought against them. Knowing your rights helps protect your work and interests when they are at risk. Equally, being aware of

---

20 *Ibid* at para 29.
21 *Ibid* at para 30.

potential claims against you is critical, as defending a claim can lead to costly legal battles, financial penalties, and damage to your reputation. This loss of trust from clients can affect future business opportunities, making it crucial to handle all legal matters carefully and professionally.

14

Risk Management Practices

To reduce the risk of legal claims and litigation, photographers should implement comprehensive risk management strategies.

Insurance Coverage

As a photographer you never know what tomorrow may bring, and having insurance to cover unexpected events is important. There are different kinds of insurance you should consider.

Liability insurance insures you against claims for physical injury or property damage resulting from your activities. This type of coverage is important if you are working on location or in your studio and there is a risk of accidents or damage occurring. The cost of insurance depends on factors such as the level of risk exposure[1] and coverage limits.

Errors and Omissions Insurance (E&O Insurance) for photographers in Canada, also known as professional liability insurance, provides protection against a variety of claims resulting in financial loss or damages to a client. E&O Insurance covers things like negligence, errors in deliverables,[2] breach of contract, libel and slander, and intellectual property infringement. The cost of E&O Insurance will vary with such factors as your level of experience, the scope of services you provide, and the coverage limits.

Equipment insurance protects against damage, loss, or theft of your photography equipment, including your camera, lenses, lighting equipment, and accessories. The cost of equipment insurance varies based on the value of your equipment, the size of the deductible, and the coverage limits.

Business interruption insurance provides coverage for lost income and expenses if your business is disrupted due to unforeseen circumstances such as fire, floods, or natural disasters. The cost of the insurance varies depending on factors such as the size of your business, the amount of coverage needed, and the risk of interruptions.

Commercial property insurance shields you against damage or loss to your studio space, equipment, and furniture. You can also get insurance to cover fire, theft, and

---

1 This includes the likelihood and severity of possible claims.

2 This includes mistakes such as delivering poor quality photographs, missing key shots at an event, or failing to meet the agreed upon deadlines.

vandalism. The cost varies depending on the value of the insured property, the location of your premises, and the coverage limits.

Written Contracts

Use written contracts for all client engagements. These should outline the scope of work, responsibilities, deliverables, timelines, payment terms, and usage rights for the photographs. This comprehensive approach ensures that all parties are fully aware of their rights and obligations, helping to prevent misunderstandings and disputes.

Administrative Practices

Getting model releases from everyone you photograph is crucial because it protects you from potential claims of privacy or publicity rights violations. A signed release form serves as a documented agreement where the subject consents to the use of their likeness for specified purposes. This prevents any disputes regarding the use of the images, whether they are for commercial, editorial, or other purposes.

Registering your copyright not only establishes legal proof of ownership but also significantly strengthens your ability to enforce your rights if infringement occurs. When your work is officially registered, it provides a documented record that can serve as evidence in court, making it easier to pursue legal action against unauthorized use of your images. Additionally, it deters potential infringers from using your work without permission, because they know that your copyright has this extra level of protection.

Keep detailed records of client interactions, contracts, releases, invoices, and correspondence. Thorough documentation is invaluable for resolving misunderstandings or disputes and supporting your position in legal claims. By maintaining organized and accessible records, you can quickly provide evidence of agreed upon terms, permissions granted, and services rendered.

Clearly communicate expectations, deliverables, and potential risks or limitations with clients and other stakeholders. Regularly sharing updates helps you tackle issues quickly and keeps everyone on the same page. This approach also builds trust and teamwork, which leads to successful projects and strong professional relationships.

By adopting these risk management practices, photographers can build a strong professional reputation, and significantly reduce the chance of legal complications.

15

Selling Your Photography Services

Photography Services Agreement

What if you are not just selling your photographs, but are also selling your services as a photographer? Success requires that both you and your client clearly understand and agree on expectations. The way to achieve this is by using a photography services agreement. A contract of this kind typically outlines the scope of services, payment terms, delivery timelines, usage rights, copyright ownership, and other important details to protect both the photographer and the client. It ensures that both parties have a clear understanding of their respective expectations and responsibilities, helping prevent disputes.

Terms of Your Engagement

It is important for the contract to set out in detail the nature of the services you will be providing in order that both parties are clear on what will be done. Include the date, time, and location, as well as other relevant details such as the type of shots you will be taking and any additional services to be provided.

Specify the type of photography, for example, wedding, portrait, or event, the duration of the shoot, and the number of photographs expected. Clearly outline any additional services, such as photo editing, creation of albums, or delivery of physical prints. Detail any special requirements or requests from the client to avoid misunderstandings.

Set out a clear timeline for the delivery of photographs. Include an initial preview date where clients can view a selection of edited images, and a final delivery date for the complete package. Specify the format of the delivery (digital files, prints, albums) and how they will be delivered (online gallery, USB, or physical delivery).

Payment Terms

Clearly state the total cost, deposit requirements, and payment schedule. Outline any additional fees for extra services or overtime. Do you want a deposit of some kind, or a non-refundable retainer that is paid when your client signs the contract? Are there any discounts, extra fees, or taxes that need to be accounted for? Ensure the client understands when payments are due and the consequences of late payments or cancellations. Consider what you want to do if your client fails to pay your bill on time or does not show up for the photo shoot.

Ownership and Usage Rights

Clarify the copyright ownership and usage rights. Copyright law is something that your client may not understand. The client could say: "I am paying you to take the photographs. Why do you own the copyright?" It is important that your client understand that under the *Copyright Act* the photographer who takes the photographs own the copyright in the photographs.

Wording should be incorporated into the contract that sets out how your client can use the photographs. Can your client use the photographs for personal use only, or can they use them commercially in some way? You can agree to allow the client permission to use the photographs in a particular way, or even sell your copyright interest to the client for a fee. The contract can also address the duration of usage, which can range up to indefinite usage.

In addition, it is essential for you to set out how you intend to use the photographs. Are you just adding them to your own portfolio, or are you permitted to share your work on your website, post them to social media, or submit them for publication in a magazine?

Cancellation and Rescheduling Policies

The contract should outline the procedures for rescheduling or cancelling the photoshoot. You can also set out any penalties or fees if your client wants to make changes to the agreed upon schedule. This protects you, the photographer, from last-minute cancellations and provides a process for handling any unforeseen changes that come up.

Confidentiality and Privacy

The agreement can address confidentiality and privacy concerns, ensuring that both parties agree on how sensitive information and images will be handled and protected.

The confidentiality clause should address several issues. Define what constitutes confidential information, including personal data and sensitive details shared during the photography process. Include a clause stating that both parties will not disclose any confidential information to third parties without prior consent by the other party. Detail how the client's personal data will be stored, protected, and processed in compliance with relevant privacy laws.

Indemnification and Liability

This type of clause outlines who is responsible in a case of damages, injuries, or losses that occur during the engagement. This helps manage the risks for both parties and ensures that both parties understand their responsibilities.

An indemnification and liability clause should define the extent of the photographer's liability for any damages or losses incurred during the provision of services. Make sure to detail the client's obligation to indemnify and hold the photographer harmless from any claims, damages, or expenses arising from the client's actions or use of the photographs. You should also include provisions that deal with third-party claims, including legal fees and costs, if they arise.

Insurance Clause

An insurance clause in a photography services agreement should clearly outline the insurance responsibilities of both the photographer and the client. The agreement should specify that the photographer must maintain adequate liability insurance to cover potential damages or accidents during the photo shoot. This includes public liability insurance to cover any third-party injury or property damage that might occur while performing the services. Similarly, the client should have insurance to cover any injuries or property damage that may occur during the event or at the location where the photography services are being provided. Additionally, the agreement should require both parties to provide proof of insurance upon request.

Force Majeure

A limitation of liability clause protects you from liability if certain things happen that are beyond your control. This would cover a situation where you are unable to complete the photo shoot because of events such as a natural disaster, illness, or injury. You should also set out whether you are prepared to complete the photo shoot later, provide a replacement photographer, or refund the client's deposit in the event of a natural disaster.

Summary

A well-structured photography services agreement offers numerous benefits, both for the photographer and the client. It provides a clear outline of the expectations, deliverables, and obligations of both parties, reducing the likelihood of misunderstandings or disputes. By defining key details such as payment terms, copyright ownership, usage rights, and cancellation policies, the contract ensures that both sides are protected legally and financially. In addition, a detailed agreement helps manage client expectations by specifying timelines for photo delivery, the number of images to be provided, and any additional services like editing or album creation.

Having a solid agreement also mitigates risks. Provisions related to indemnification, liability, and insurance protect the photographer from unexpected liabilities, such as damages or accidents during the shoot. Meanwhile, clauses like *force majeure* safeguard both parties in case of unforeseen events, such as illness or natural disasters, that may prevent the shoot from proceeding as planned.

In conclusion, a comprehensive photography services agreement is essential for fostering clear communication, protecting legal interests, and ensuring a smooth, professional relationship between the photographer and the client.

16

Marketing Your Photographs

Marketing your photographs effectively is crucial for establishing a successful career in photography. In today's digital age, there are a variety of strategies you can employ to reach your target audience, build a strong brand, and generate income from your work. Here are some examples.

Stock Photograph Websites

Stock photography websites like Shutterstock, Adobe Stock, and Getty Images have a massive global user base. By placing your images on these platforms, you gain exposure to a worldwide audience. This can significantly increase the visibility of your work, attracting not only buyers but also potential clients for commissioned work. The international reach allows your photographs to be used in various industries across different countries, enhancing your portfolio's diversity and recognition.

One of the biggest advantages of stock photography is the potential to generate ongoing income from a single photograph. Each time your image is licensed, you earn a royalty, creating a passive income stream. Over time, as you upload more images and they gain traction, this can lead to a substantial and consistent revenue source, especially as you build a diverse collection of high-demand images.

Stock photography websites offer an accessible way for photographers at all levels to monetize their work. You do not need to have a professional studio or high-end equipment to start earning. If you have quality images that meet the platform's standards, you can begin uploading and selling your work. This low entry requirement makes it easier for photographers to start earning money without a significant upfront investment.

Social Media Marketing

Social media platforms like Instagram, Facebook, Pinterest, and X (formerly known as Twitter) have vast global user bases, offering unparalleled visibility for your work. By sharing your photographs on these platforms, you can reach a broad and diverse audience, including potential clients, collaborators, and fans. Social media algorithms can amplify your reach, especially if your content is engaging and resonates with users, potentially leading to viral exposure.

Social media allows for direct interaction with your audience. You can receive immediate feedback through comments, likes, and shares, helping you gauge the impact of your work. Engaging with your followers by responding to comments or messages builds a community around your photography, fostering loyalty and encouraging word-of-mouth promotion. This interaction also provides valuable insights into what your audience likes, guiding your creative direction.

Marketing using social media is also a cost-effective way to promote your work. Creating accounts and sharing content is free, making it accessible even for photographers with limited budgets. While there are options for paid advertising, which can further boost your reach, growth through strategic content sharing and engagement can be highly effective without any financial investment.

Leverage the Public Domain

The public domain is a collection of creative works, such as books, music, art, and photographs that are no longer protected by copyright or where the creator has waived their rights, allowing anyone to use, modify, and distribute the works freely without permission or payment.

Because photographs are free of copyright protection, anyone can use them without needing to seek permission or pay licensing fees. This can make your work available to a wider range of users who might otherwise avoid copyrighted material due to legal complexities or costs, further increasing your visibility. Educational institutions, researchers, artists, and content creators are more likely to use public domain images because they are free and come without legal restrictions. This can dramatically increase the visibility of your work across different platforms, projects, and industries, leading to broader recognition.

Create a Professional Website

Having your own website gives you complete control over how your work is presented and how your brand is perceived. You can customize the design, layout, and content to reflect your unique style and vision, which helps establish a strong and consistent brand identity. Unlike social media platforms or third-party galleries, your website allows you to showcase your portfolio exactly the way you want, without restrictions or advertisements.

Your website serves as a hub for direct communication with potential clients. You can include contact forms, booking systems, and live chat options that make it easy for clients to reach out to you, ask questions, and book your services. This direct engagement can lead to higher conversion rates, as clients appreciate the convenience and personal touch of interacting with you directly.

Unlike social media platforms, where your work is often displayed in a feed alongside other content, your website allows you to showcase your entire portfolio in a curated and organized manner. You can categorize your work by genre, project, or client, making it easier for visitors to explore your photography and get a comprehensive view of your skills and experience.

Market Your Photographs Through Galleries and Public Spaces

You can partner with art galleries to showcase your work. Many galleries have open calls for submissions or offer exhibition spaces for emerging photographers. Some may take a commission from sales, while others may charge a fee to display your work.

You can also display your photographs in non-traditional venues like cafés, restaurants, community centres, or corporate spaces. These locations often host rotating art displays and allow photographers to showcase their work to a broader audience who may not typically visit art galleries.

Attending gallery openings and public exhibitions where your work is displayed helps you connect with potential buyers, collectors, or collaborators. This can be invaluable for building your reputation in the photography community.

Many galleries and public spaces now include online promotions as part of their exhibits. Having your work displayed online, in addition to physical spaces, can boost visibility and attract potential buyers from a broader geographic area.

17
Social and Ethical Considerations

Overview

Photography holds the power to shape perspectives and affect the lives of those captured in an image. You must be conscious of the social impact your work can have on people and communities. By respecting cultural differences, honouring privacy rights, and adhering to ethical standards, you not only tell authentic stories but also ensure that your work promotes understanding, fairness, and respect for all individuals involved.

Respecting the Privacy and Dignity of People

Photographers need to think about the impact of their work. This involves considering how their images might affect the people they photograph, as well as viewers and society more generally.

Respect for a person's privacy is crucial, particularly in those situations where they are vulnerable or in distress. For instance, consider a woman who has stepped away from a serious car accident scene and is visibly upset. Capturing her image could tell a powerful story about the tragedy's impact. However, photographing her without her consent in her fragile state might cause more harm.

Photographers need to balance the importance of the photograph against the possible negative effects on the individual. In her fragile state, asking for her permission might only cause more discomfort. In this instance, refraining from taking the photograph is the right approach, placing greater value on her privacy and dignity, than capturing a powerful but invasive image.

Vulnerable Populations

When photographing vulnerable individuals, such as those experiencing homelessness or facing difficult circumstances, photographers should avoid exploiting their situation. It is essential to approach these subjects with empathy and respect, considering the potential harm that could result from misrepresentation or insensitive use of their images. In many cases, individuals in vulnerable situations may not be able to give informed consent, and their dignity must be prioritized above all. Ensure that images taken do not perpetuate harmful stereotypes or further marginalize these individuals. By ensuring that the images are used to raise awareness and promote compassion photographers can contribute positively to social understanding without causing harm.

Cultural Sensitivity

Photographers also need to be sensitive to cultural differences when they are photographing people from diverse backgrounds. For example, a tourist visiting a foreign country may have the opportunity to take photographs of people and events during a colourful religious ceremony. However, without understanding the cultural significance of the ceremony, or obtaining consent from the subjects, this may be considered disrespectful. It is also important to ensure you do not misrepresent cultural groups in some way that will perpetuate harmful stereotypes.

Be mindful of how your presence and actions affect those around you. Always put the comfort and dignity of your subjects first, capturing their image in a way that reflects who they are. Be considerate. This will help build trust, create meaningful connections, and produce more genuine and powerful images.

Indigenous Cultures

Historically, Indigenous Peoples have been photographed and portrayed in ways that perpetuate harmful stereotypes, either romanticizing or marginalizing their communities. This has contributed to the ongoing misrepresentation of their identity in mainstream culture. Photographers today have a responsibility to ensure that their images of Indigenous individuals and communities are respectful and accurate, portraying them in a way that reflects their real experiences and perspectives. This requires sensitivity to the cultural, social, and historical factors that shape the environment where the photographs are taken.

In some Indigenous cultures, photography is not just a neutral act but can be seen as intrusive or disrespectful, especially if it captures sacred ceremonies or private moments without permission. For example, certain rituals or ceremonies may be sacred and not meant to be viewed or documented by outsiders. Photographers need to be aware that what might seem like a compelling shot could violate cultural taboos or spiritual beliefs. By seeking permission, the photographer demonstrates respect for Indigenous cultural practices.

Accuracy and Truthfulness

Photographers should focus on capturing images that reflect reality and avoid manipulating them in ways that mislead viewers or distort the truth. Maintaining the integrity of the image is key. Minor edits, like colour adjustments or cropping, are acceptable, but altering the content to change the context or misrepresent the subject breaks the trust between the photographer and the audience.

By sticking to these standards, photographers show respect for their subjects and ensure their images truthfully represent the moment. This builds credibility and fosters trust with the audience, who can rely on the images as honest representations. This is especially important in fields like photojournalism, where photographs often document real-world events and influence public opinion. Staying committed to truthfulness helps photography remain a trusted and respected form of communication.

Representation and Diversity

Recording the diversity of Canadian society through photography is important for several reasons. It creates a visual record of the country's many cultures, traditions, and histories, helping people understand and appreciate Canada's multicultural identity. By showcasing the lives and contributions of different communities, photographers highlight how different perspectives have shaped the nation. This kind of photography promotes a more accurate portrayal of Canadian life, pushing back against biases. Photography also becomes a way to help drive social change, ultimately strengthening the connections among Canadians.

18

Staying Up to Date

As a photographer, how do you keep yourself informed about emerging issues that may affect your rights and obligations? Keeping up to date is essential and there are several ways you can do this.

To stay informed on photography law and intellectual property matters, consider subscribing to specialized publications, websites, and blogs that cover topics like updates to the *Copyright Act* and recent court cases.[1] Staying current with laws, regulations, and industry standards related to copyright, privacy, and advertising can help you avoid legal issues and ensure compliance. Keeping up with legislative changes and best practices also enhances your credibility and

---

1 CanLII (Canadian Legal Information Institute) is a non-profit organization managed by the Federation of Law Societies of Canada that allows you to search for and access court decisions from across Canada for free, online: https://www.canlii.org.

professionalism. For specific legal questions, consult a lawyer with expertise in intellectual property and copyright law.[2]

Joining professional organization and associations[3] is a very helpful way to stay up to date. Organizations of this kind may offer seminars on various legal topics that are important to your business as a photographer.

You should be aware of and utilize the Canadian Intellectual Property Office (CIPO), which is a government agency that administers intellectual property rights in Canada. CIPO provides copyright registration services, and in addition, offers a variety of resources on copyright law, including guides and educational materials on how to protect your intellectual property rights, as well as guides, resources, and tools for understanding and protecting intellectual property.

Photography clubs across Canada play a vital role in helping photographers stay current with the latest trends, techniques, and technological advancements in the field. These clubs foster a sense of community among photography

---

2 In Ontario, you can contact the Law Society of Ontario Referral Service directly at 1-855-947-5255 or 416-947-5255 (within the GTA), Monday–Friday, between 9:00 a.m.–5:00 p.m., online: https://lso.ca/public-resources/finding-a-lawyer-or-paralegal/law-society-referral-service. Other provinces will have similar services.

3 Professional Photographers of Canada (PPOC) is a national association that represents professional photographers in Canada, online: https://www.ppoc.ca. They offer various resources, including workshops, seminars, and certification programs to help photographers stay current on industry standards and legal issues. Also consider Canadian Association of Professional Image Creators (CAPIC), online: https://capic.org/. CAPIC is a national association that supports photographers, illustrators, and other image creators. They provide networking opportunities, educational resources, and advocacy on copyright and business practices.

enthusiasts, providing a space for members to share knowledge, critique each other's work, and learn from experienced photographers. Regular workshops, guest speakers, and hands-on sessions keep members informed about new equipment, software, and methods, ensuring that they remain innovative in their craft.[4]

In conclusion, actively participating in professional associations, using the Canadian Intellectual Property Office's tools, connecting with photography clubs, and staying informed through relevant publications and legal updates will equip you to skilfully handle the complexities of the industry and achieve success.

4 To find photography clubs in Canada, you can visit the Canadian Association for Photographic Art (CAPA) website, online: https://capacanada.ca/. CAPA offers a directory of affiliated photography clubs across the country, making it easier to locate a club near you.

Appendix 1: Photograph Assignment Agreement

This Photograph Assignment Agreement (the "Agreement") is made and entered into as of [Date], by and between:

Assignor: [Assignor's Name], with a principal address at [Assignor's Address], and
Assignee: [Assignee's Name], with a principal address at [Assignee's Address].

1. **ASSIGNMENT OF RIGHTS**
   1.1 The Assignor hereby transfers and assigns to the Assignee all rights, title, and interest, including copyright, in and to the following photographs (the "Assigned Photographs"): [Describe the photographs, e.g., specific images, series, or collection].
   1.2 The Assignor also waives any moral rights to the Assigned Photographs, as permitted under the **Copyright Act of Canada**.

1.3 The Assignee shall have full ownership of the Assigned Photographs, including the right to reproduce, distribute, modify, display, and sublicense them in any format or medium.

2. **COMPENSATION**

2.1 In exchange for the rights granted under this Agreement, the Assignee shall pay the Assignor the sum of [Amount] CAD, payable [Payment Terms, e.g., upon signing, per image, in instalments].

2.2 The Assignor acknowledges that upon receipt of payment, they no longer hold any rights to the Assigned Photographs.

3. **WARRANTIES AND REPRESENTATIONS**

3.1 The Assignor represents and warrants that: (a) They are the sole owner of the Assigned Photographs and have full authority to transfer ownership; (b) The Assigned Photographs do not infringe upon the rights of any third party; (c) No other agreements exist that would conflict with this Assignment; (d) The photographs do not violate any privacy laws or contain defamatory content under Canadian law.

4. **INDEMNIFICATION**

4.1 The Assignor agrees to indemnify and hold the Assignee harmless from any claims, disputes, or liabilities arising from a breach of the warranties stated in this Agreement.

5. **GOVERNING LAW**

5.1 This Agreement shall be governed by and interpreted in accordance with the laws of the province of [Province] and the applicable federal laws of Canada, including the **Copyright Act** and **Personal Information Protection and Electronic Documents Act (PIPEDA)** where applicable.

5.2 Any disputes related to this Agreement shall be resolved in the courts of [Province].

6. **GENERAL PROVISIONS**

6.1 **Entire Agreement:** This Agreement constitutes the entire understanding between the parties and supersedes all prior agreements.

6.2 **Amendments:** Any modifications must be in writing and signed by both parties.

6.3 **Severability:** If any provision is found invalid, the remainder of the Agreement shall remain in effect.

6.4 **Waiver:** Failure to enforce any provision shall not constitute a waiver of rights.

6.5 **Further Assurances:** The Assignor agrees to execute any further documents required to perfect the Assignee's ownership rights.

IN WITNESS WHEREOF, the parties have executed this Agreement as of the date first written above.

Assignor:
Signature: ______________________
Name: _________________________
Date: __________________________

Assignor:
Signature: ______________________
Name: _________________________
Date: __________________________

Appendix 2: Photography Licensing Agreement

This Photography Licensing Agreement (the "Agreement") is made and entered into as of [Date], by and between:

Licensor: [Licensor's Name], with a principal address at [Licensor's Address], and
Licensee: [Licensee's Name], with a principal address at [Licensee's Address].

1. GRANT OF LICENCE

1.1 The Licensor grants the Licensee a [non-exclusive/exclusive], [revocable/irrevocable], [transferable/non-transferable], [worldwide/territory-specific] licence to use the following photographs (the "Licensed Photographs"): [Describe the licensed photographs, e.g., specific images, series, or collection].

1.2 The Licensee may use the Licensed Photographs solely for the following purpose(s): [Specify permitted uses, e.g., commercial, editorial, personal use].

2. RESTRICTIONS

2.1 The Licensee shall not: (a) Modify, alter, or create derivative works of the Licensed Photographs without prior written consent; (b) Transfer, sublicense, or distribute the Licensed Photographs to any third party without approval; (c) Use the Licensed Photographs for any unlawful, defamatory, obscene, or infringing purposes; (d) Claim ownership of the Licensed Photographs or remove any copyright or attribution notices.

3. COMPENSATION

3.1 In consideration for the rights granted under this Agreement, the Licensee shall pay the Licensor a licensing fee of [Amount] CAD, payable [Payment Terms, e.g., upon signing, per usage, monthly, annually].

3.2 Late payments shall incur interest at a rate of [Specify Interest Rate] per month.

4. TERM AND TERMINATION

4.1 This Agreement shall commence on [Start Date] and remain in effect until [End Date] or until terminated by either party in accordance with this section.

4.2 Either party may terminate this Agreement with [Notice Period] written notice if the other party breaches any material term and fails to remedy the breach within [Cure Period].

4.3 Upon termination, the Licensee shall cease using and destroy all copies of the Licensed Photographs.

5. INTELLECTUAL PROPERTY RIGHTS

5.1 The Licensor retains all rights, title, and interest in the Licensed Photographs, including all copyright and moral rights. Nothing in this Agreement transfers ownership of the Licensed Photographs to the Licensee.

5.2 The Licensee shall provide proper attribution to the Licensor where required, using the following format: [Specify attribution format, if applicable].

6. WARRANTIES AND LIABILITY

6.1 The Licensor represents that they have the legal right to grant this licence and that the Licensed Photographs do not infringe any third-party rights.

6.2 The Licensed Photographs are provided "as is," without warranties of any kind. The Licensor shall not be liable for any indirect, incidental, or consequential damages arising from this Agreement.

7. INDEMNIFICATION

7.1 The Licensee agrees to indemnify and hold the Licensor harmless from any claims, liabilities, or expenses arising from the Licensee's use of the Licensed Photographs.

8. GOVERNING LAW

8.1 This Agreement follows the laws of the Province of [Province] and the applicable federal laws of Canada.

8.2 Any disagreements related to this Agreement will be handled in the courts of [Province].

9. GENERAL PROVISIONS

9.1 **Entire Agreement:** This Agreement constitutes the entire understanding between the parties and supersedes all prior agreements.

9.2 **Amendments:** Any modifications must be in writing and signed by both parties.

9.3 **Severability:** If any provision is found invalid, the remainder of the Agreement shall remain in effect.

9.4 **Waiver:** Failure to enforce any provision shall not constitute a waiver of rights.

IN WITNESS WHEREOF, the parties have executed this Agreement as of the date first written above.

Licensor:
Signature: ______________________
Name: ______________________
Date: ______________________

Licensee:
Signature: ______________________
Name: ______________________
Date: ______________________

Appendix 3: Photography Release Agreement

This Photography Release Agreement (the "Agreement") is made and entered into as of [Date], by and between:

Releasor: [Releasor's Name], with a principal address at [Releasor's Address], and
Releasee: [Releasee's Name], with a principal address at [Releasee's Address].

1. **GRANT OF RIGHTS**
   1.1 The Releasor hereby grants the Releasee, their representatives, assigns, and licensees, the irrevocable and unrestricted right to use, reproduce, modify, publish, distribute, and publicly display photographs featuring the Releasor (the "Released Photographs") in any format or medium, for lawful purposes including but

not limited to advertising, marketing, social media, editorial, and commercial use.

1.2 The Releasor acknowledges that they have no further rights, title, or interest in the Released Photographs, including any right to compensation, unless otherwise specified in this Agreement.

2. **WAIVER OF CLAIMS**

2.1 The Releasor waives any and all claims, demands, or causes of action against the Releasee, its employees, affiliates, and assigns, arising from or relating to the use of the Released Photographs, including but not limited to claims for defamation, invasion of privacy, or misappropriation of likeness.

2.2 The Releasor acknowledges that the Released Photographs may be altered, combined with other images, or used in any manner the Releasee deems appropriate, provided such use does not violate any applicable laws.

3. **REPRESENTATIONS AND WARRANTIES**

3.1 The Releasor represents and warrants that: (a) They are over the age of majority in their province/territory of residence, or have obtained the consent of their parent or legal guardian; (b) They have the legal authority to grant the rights set forth in this Agreement; (c) The execution of this Agreement does not violate the rights of any third party.

4. **COMPENSATION (IF APPLICABLE)**

4.1 If compensation is agreed upon, the Releasee shall pay the Releasor the sum of [Amount] CAD, payable

[Payment Terms, e.g., upon signing, upon publication, per image].

4.2 If no compensation is provided, the Releasor acknowledges that they are granting this release voluntarily and without expectation of payment.

5. **GOVERNING LAW**

5.1 This Agreement shall be governed by and construed in accordance with the laws of the Province of [Province] and the applicable federal laws of Canada, including the **Copyright Act** and **Personal Information Protection and Electronic Documents Act (PIPEDA)** where applicable.

5.2 Any disputes related to this Agreement shall be resolved in the courts of [Province].

6. **GENERAL PROVISIONS**

6.1 **Entire Agreement:** This Agreement constitutes the entire understanding between the parties and supersedes all prior agreements.

6.2 **Amendments:** Any modifications must be in writing and signed by both parties.

6.3 **Severability:** If any provision is found invalid, the remainder of the Agreement shall remain in effect.

6.4 **Waiver:** Failure to enforce any provision shall not constitute a waiver of rights.

IN WITNESS WHEREOF, the parties have executed this Agreement as of the date first written above.

Releasor:
Signature: ______________________
Name: ______________________
Date: ______________________

Releasee:
Signature: ______________________
Name: ______________________
Date: ______________________

Appendix 4: Cease and Desist Notice

[Your Name or Business Name]
[Your Address]
[City, Province, Postal Code]
[Your Email]
[Your Phone Number]
[Date]

VIA [Email/Mail/Registered Mail]
[Recipient's Name]
[Recipient's Address]
[City, Province, Postal Code]

Subject: Cease and Desist – Unauthorized Use of [Describe Issue, e.g., Copyrighted Photographs]

Dear [Recipient's Name],
This letter serves as a formal **Cease and Desist** notice regarding the unauthorized use of [Describe the Work, e.g., specific

photographs] owned by [Your Name or Business Name]. It has come to my attention that you have used, reproduced, distributed, or otherwise exploited these materials without my explicit permission, in violation of my legal rights under **Canadian law, including the Copyright Act**.

Immediate Actions Required:

1. **Cease and desist** all unauthorized use, reproduction, distribution, or display of the specified works immediately.
2. **Remove and destroy** all copies of the unauthorized materials from any digital or physical locations.
3. **Provide written confirmation** within [X] days of receipt of this letter that you have complied with the above demands.

Failure to comply with this demand may result in legal action, including but not limited to seeking damages, injunctive relief, and legal costs. This letter does not waive any rights or remedies available under law, and I expressly reserve the right to take further legal action if necessary.

I encourage you to resolve this matter amicably. Please confirm compliance by responding in writing to the address or email provided above.

Sincerely,

[Your Name]
[Your Business Name, if applicable]
[Your Contact Information]

Table of Cases

Index

has also contributed to legal education as an instructor at Osgoode Hall Law School's Intensive Trial Advocacy Program, the University of Toronto's internationally trained lawyers' program, and presented papers at various legal conferences. He retired on 31 August 2022.

In addition to his legal career, Robert is an experienced amateur photographer, giving him a unique perspective on the intersection of photography and the law. His passion for photography, combined with his interest in and understanding of the legal principles, makes him well-suited to author a comprehensive resource addressing the laws that apply to photography in Canada.

About the Author

Robert Ratcliffe is an experienced legal counsel with more than three decades working at Ontario's Ministry of the Attorney General Crown Law Office – Civil, where he served as counsel in a broad range of civil litigation matters. His extensive career includes representing the provincial Crown at all levels of court, including the Supreme Court of Canada. During that time, he acted as counsel on a large variety of files, including large class action proceedings, judicial reviews, and Indigenous land claims.

Robert holds an LLM from Osgoode Hall Law School, an LLB from the University of Ottawa, and a BA from Western University (previously known as University of Wester Ontario). His commitment to legal education over the ye is reflected in his active involvement with the Ontario Association, where he has organized and co-chaired grams on administrative law and privacy issues. R